# How to Whittle the Whimsies of Yesterday

## Jack D. Jackson

NORTEX PRESS  Austin, Texas

FIRST EDITION
Copyright © 2005
By Jack D. Jackson
Published in the United States of America
By Nortex Press
A Division of Sunbelt Media, Inc.
P.O. Drawer 90159 🏠 Austin, Texas 78709-0159
email: sales@eakinpress.com
💻 website: www.eakinpress.com 💻
ALL RIGHTS RESERVED.
1   2   3   4   5   6   7   8   9
**ISBN 978-1-57168-996-2**
**ISBN 1-57168-996-6**
Library of Congress Control Number 2005932003

# Contents

# Introduction

I dedicate this book to my wonderful wife, partner, mother of three kids and grandmother to half a handful, and maybe two handfuls in time to come. I owe her more thanks than words could ever say for putting up with me for almost forty years.

After we had been married for twenty-five years, she instilled in me the thing I loved to do most when I was a kid. That was to "whittle." One thing I liked

*Airplane propeller*

to make was a propeller-on-a-stick, like the one shown here.

I would wire and tape these little windmills onto my bicycle and ride as fast as my legs would pedal just to create enough wind to make it turn. It was pure magic when it did! Needless to say, I was getting a lot of exercise watching my invention work. I made some big, some small and even began to think about making one big enough to pull my bicycle along just like an airplane, by somehow making it turn with the pedals. I thought about this for a few years until bigger and better things came along. Things like learning to drive a tractor or my daddy's pickup truck. Before long there were still more things beginning to happen that would keep my mind off of whittling. There was school, of course, and grass to mow, ballgames to play, fish to catch, buddies to hang out with, and girls, like the ones who came home with my sisters for the weekends.

"Girls"! Can you believe that girls could somehow keep a boy's mind off of whittling?

As it turned out, I never got around to doing any serious whittling until my wife and I had been married long enough to raise three kids, put them through school and out on their own. That's when the whittling bug hit me again. I suppose it had been there all along, it just took my loving wife to bring it back into full bloom.

I came home from work one day about fifteen years ago, and my wife was looking through a magazine. She said to me, "Would you look at this cute whimsy." Of course I didn't know what she was talking about so I asked, "What is a whimsy?" She told me it was a ball in a cage with a chain, all whittled from one piece of wood. "I bet the man who did this really knows how to whittle!" Well this sounded just like the things I had made as a kid! She asked, "Do you think you could whittle me one to put on the fireplace mantel?" I replied, "If I did, you probably wouldn't want anyone to see it." There was nothing else said about whimsies, but she sure had me thinking and wondering if I could whittle one of those for her. I got started whittling on sticks, just getting the feel of the knife after so many years, and trying

to figure out how someone could actually whittle a ball inside of a cage? I found a 2"×4" piece of white pine and sawed a few pieces off that were 1" square and 5-6" long. After three failed attempts, I finally accomplished my first whimsy. (shown here)

*My first Whimsey*

I brought it in the house and said to my wife, "Is this close to what you had in mind?" She said, "Oh my goodness, you made me a whimsy, just like the one in the magazine!" Well, that really made me feel good, so maybe it wasn't so bad after all. By this time I had a severe case of "whittling fever" and started another one right away.

While showing this whimsy, which is also made out of pine, I realized I couldn't remember when I had made it. That is when I realized that I needed to date and sign my work, and I advise everyone to do that.

By now, I had taken to whittling like a duck takes to water. I could not wait to get in my easy chair, knife in hand, a towel across my lap (to catch the shavings) and the evening news on TV. I was looking forward to three hours of pure pleasure. I soon learned the hard way that a common pocket knife will fold over on you and cut your finger right down to the bone. It is almost impossible to whittle when this happens, until it heals up. After nearly cutting my finger off, I started thinking about safety. I went shopping at a local woodcarving store and learned that I could buy a safety glove, thumbguards and knives that locked. I spent almost $100 that day buying these items and spent the rest of my recuperation time sharpening the new knives. The new knives didn't all work for me. The first one was the interchangeable blade-type, which just didn't suit my kind of whittling and another one, which they claim was made especially for carving, didn't work for me either.

The third knife, which I bought at a local hardware store, worked after some minor adjustments. It was a small knife with a single carbon steel blade that locked. It is an Old Timer 18 0T pocket knife. The handle was too small, so I sandwiched it in wood. The blade was too long so I cut it off to measure 1¼" long. I then sharpened it with a coarse Diamond Stone and rounded the point to suit me.

While knife shopping that day, I discovered Bass wood is the wood of choice for woodcarvers the world over and then later, I found another wood, Aspen, which is fairly nice to carve. The chain in a log with two balls (shown below) is made out of Aspen wood. Notice the small brown spots on the two balls and one of the chain links.

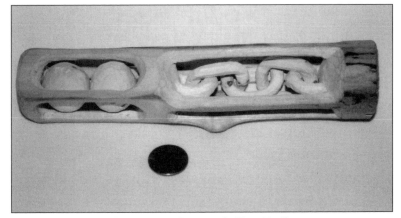

*Chain in a Log with Two Balls*

The brown spots are the core of the Aspen wood and that is the only thing I have against it. On a bigger log, you can get a piece on either side of the core. I have already told you about that first bad accident when my knife folded over and cut my finger and I can't stress enough how important it is to wear a safety glove on the hand holding the work piece. I have slipped with my knife before, and jabbed a hole in the hand that is holding the piece I was working on. So always remember that safety and common sense will help prevent serious injuries.

Of all the carvings I have done in the last fifteen years this little slender pyramid is my wife's favorite. (shown here). It came about by accident. It was a sliver of Bass wood sawed off from a larger piece. One day I wanted to whittle, so I rummaged through my box of scrap wood and found this little splinter. I started smoothing it up with my knife, not really sure what I was going to make with it. After whit-

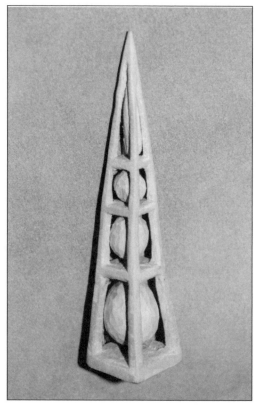

*My wife's favorite whimsy*

tling it to a sharp point, I began to imagine that there might be a ball hidden inside this little triangle. I started at the bottom and whittled the evening away making the larger ball. The next evening, I pondered through Dan Rather's newscast, not knowing what to whittle next. It hit me. I couldn't make the slender bars without a partition between each ball. This would give each ball its own cage, therefore giving strength to the slender fragile bars. As it turned out, there was a Teardrop Ball, a Baby Ball, a Mama Ball and a Daddy Ball. All of that from this little scrap wood! Some of my favorite pieces come from that scrap box. The most creative and odd shapes happen by accident. I recommend that you don't throw away anything bigger than your finger in case you might want to make a tiny whimsy that will probably turn out to be cute and someone's favorite piece.

The knives I use for these projects will be shown in detail and in their own specific applications. I will also show you how to reshape blades to make them suit each project in this book and explain how to use the grinder and whetstones.

If you do not have easy access to Bass wood or Aspen wood, you can find a piece of soft white Pine at your local lumber yard to start with. The closer the grain is the better. Practice by doing some basic whittling before launching into a project like a chain or a ball in a cage. You can start by making a square stick round and then put a point on it. If your practice wood has a knot or two, you will notice that they are harder to whittle and learn that you can enhance these knots by making eyes or noses out of them. Just use your imagination and what you end up with will probably be a one of a kind.

Try whittling out a doughnut that could be worn as a bracelet, a simple wooden heart or maybe a wooden spoon or fork. Soon you can whittle whatever you can imagine or dream up.

The first projects in this book are the easy ones to get you started in the right direction. I will close this introduction with a saying that I have heard all my life, "Only God can make a tree." So let's get started and make the best out of what God gave us. After all, life without trees would be downright boring for us whittlers!

Happy whittling and may you find as many hours of peace and contentment as I have in your new hobby.

JACK D. JACKSON

*Ball and Chain with a Hook*

# Knives and Sharpening

I could never find a blade shaped the way I wanted it or a handle that fit my hand, so converting a pocket knife into a whittling knife evolved over several years. I first started reshaping the blades of various kinds of lock blade knives, but soon found out that my hand grew tired of holding a handle that didn't fit. I then started experimenting with handles. Little by little and dozens of trials and errors, I finally had a collection of knives that would whittle anything I wanted to whittle.

I grew up when carbon steel blades were all there was, so I am still partial to them. However, the stainless steel blades available now are very good.

When making knives, I like the blade to be no longer than 1¼" Some of the smaller blades are only ½" long and ⅛" wide. Some things require round points and other projects need sharp points.

Fig. #1 This is a 3¾" long, ¾" × ½" block, any hardwood will do. I have sawed the block into two ¼" thick pieces.

Fig. #2 I have placed the knife on the block and traced the shape of the knife and the blade, then I made a straight-in cut on the line about ⅛" deep to outline the cavity for the knife.

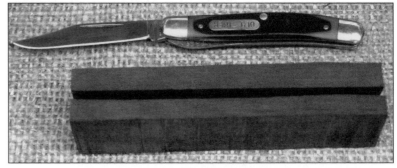
*Fig. #1*

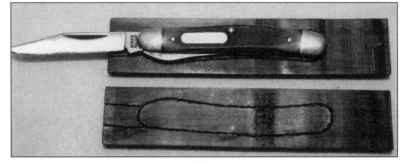
*Fig. #2*

Fig. #3: With a small gouge, I have hollowed out a cavity for the knife. I used a ⅛" gouge with a #3 curve to make this cavity. The straight-in cut you made on the lines will have to be deepened each time you gouge out to the depth of the straight-in cut.

In Fig. #4: As you deepen the cavity, place the handles around the knife, trying them on for size, so as not to get the cavity too deep. The blade being tapered means you will have to make the cavity a little deeper to accommodate the thicker part of the blade.

Work slow and take just a little out of each side. The handles should not completely touch, so that when you clamp it together in a vise it will hold the knife very firmly. Try the handle on for size and make sure it fits snugly.

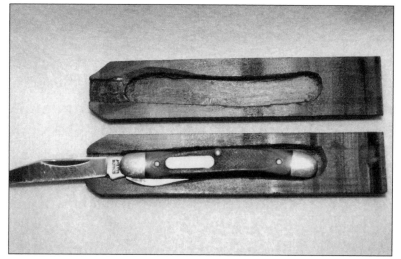
Fig. #4

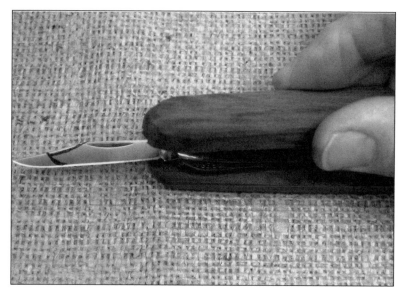
Fig. #4-A

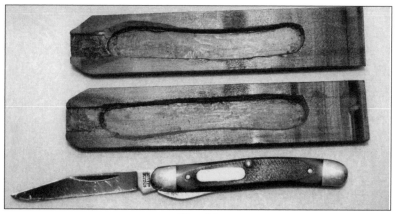
Fig. #3

I have marked the blade where the cut will be made. Mark the blade 1¼" long from the wooden handle to where the point will be.

Fig. #5 and 6: I like to cut and shape the blade before I epoxy the handle around the knife. With a cut-off wheel in a rotary tool, along with a cup of water to cool the blade, cut only 3 seconds and then plunge the blade into water to cool it. Repeat this procedure, cutting no more than 3 seconds at a time and cooling it until the cut is made.

Fig. #7: Shows the cut is made.

Fig. #8: With an extra coarse whetstone, shape the blade until you have the point rounded like the one shown here. After you have the rough shape, epoxy the knife between the wooden handles.

*Fig. #6*

*Fig #7*

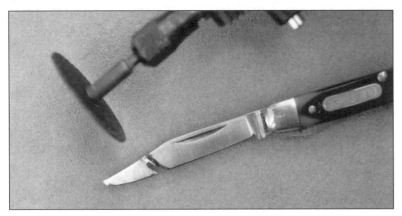
*Fig. #5*

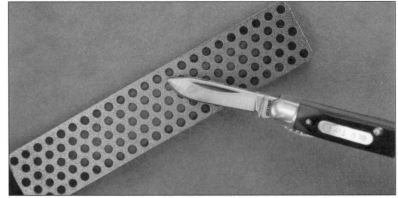
*Fig. #8*

**How to Whittle the Whimsies of Yesterday**

*Fig. #9*

*Fig. #9-A*

Fig. #9: You will need a vise similar to this small 4" one I have here or a clamp which will press the two halves firmly around the knife. The knife should be centered up in the vise, better than in these two photos. I have placed the knife this way so that it would show up better in the picture.

Using 2-ton epoxy (the 30-minute set), mix up about a teaspoon full and smear it generously on the inside of each half. Place the knife in the cavity, put the two halves back together and clamp tightly for at least 24 hours. You can say goodbye to your little knife as it will be forever entombed in wood.

Fig. #9A: The epoxy will squeeze out and drip off so place a paper towel under the knife to catch the drip. The excess epoxy can be ground off when you shape the wooden handle with a sanding wheel.

*Fig. #10*

*Fig. #11*

*Fig. #12*

*Fig. #13*

Fig. #10: When the epoxy has cured for 24 hours, you can shape the blade with a sanding wheel in the rotary tool, but the blade must still be kept cool.

Fig. #11: The handle can also be shaped with a sanding wheel. I like to make the grip fit my hand. This is more comfortable and safer, since it will grip without slipping. I never paint or varnish the wood since that would make it slick.

When putting a blade in a wooden handle, the procedure is the same except that the cavity will not be as deep and if you are using a pocket knife blade, it will have a hole for a pin which will secure the handle to the blade and make it much stronger.

Fig. #12: Making the handle for the blade and cutting the cavity. Be sure the handle fits very tight around the blade.

Fig. #13: With the blade resting snuggly in the cavity and a drill bit the same size as the hole in the blade, drill the hole through the handle half. Place the handle half without the hole on top of the blade and the handle half with the hole. Make sure the two halves fit tightly around the blade.

**How to Whittle the Whimsies of Yesterday**

*Fig. #14*

Fig. #14: Turn the assembled parts over. The handle half with the hole will now be on top. (The cutting edge of the blade in Figs. 13 and 14 are facing in opposite directions.) The drill bit will now go through the hole and the blade, for the continuation cut through the handle half on bottom.

Fig. #15: Insert the pin though the hole in the two halves and the blade, then cut it short enough so as to be below the surface of the wood on both sides, otherwise you cannot clamp it in the vise. Brass or silver pins of various sizes can be bought at knife making supply stores, but nails are cheaper and work just as well unless you want the look of silver or brass.

Fig. #16: Take the halves apart and coat each with two-ton epoxy. I like the 30-minute set as opposed to the 5-minute set as it gives you more time to work with it. Put the pin in the hole and clamp it for 24 hours. Shape the handle with the sanding wheel as we did in Fig. #11. This knife is "the big knife" in my knife collection.

*Fig. #15*

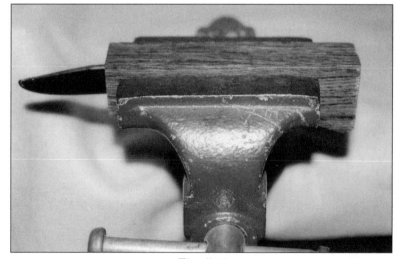

*Fig. #16*

If it breaks your heart to encase your knife in wood, never to be seen again as it did mine, I have a solution. You will need a scroll saw for this type of handle. In Fig. #17 I have an Ash block of wood 3¾" × ½" × ¾", or any hard wood would work. Draw the shape of the knife on the block and drill a hole so that you can get the scroll saw blade through it. In Fig. #18, saw around the lines and remove the wood. Now draw a line where the pencil is pointing and saw the block into two equal halves. In Fig. #19, I have marked the place where the cavity for the blade will be. In Fig. #20 the cavities for the blade are cut on both halves. The cavity on the top half is shaded and the blade is marked 1¼" long and ready to be cut. Use the same cutting and cooling technique as in Figs. #5 and 6 and then shape the blade as shown in Fig. #10.

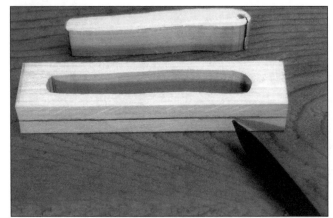

Fig. #18

Fig. #19

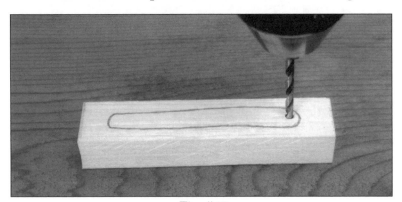

Fig. #17

Fig. #20

How to Whittle the Whimsies of Yesterday

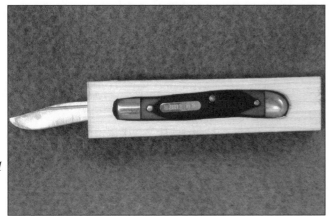

*Fig. #21*

*Fig. #22*

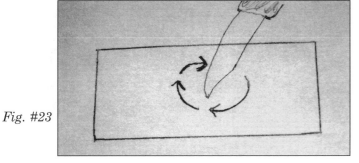

*Fig. #23*

In Fig. #21 the handles are ready to be epoxyed and clamped. You may want to shape and sharpen the blade before you epoxy it together. While the epoxy is drying, let's talk about sharpening.

Fig. #22 is a X-coarse 220 grit diamond stone which will cut the metal away very fast. I use the circular motion as in Fig. #23, holding the blade at a 20-25 degree angle to the stone, changing sides of the blade every 10-12 rotations. Shape the blade to a rounded point as in Figs. #21 and 22. This is the best shape for all-around whittling. The blade should be no longer than 1⅛" to 1¼" long for the kind of whittling I like to do. When you have the shape you want, change to a medium coarse stone and use the same motion as shown here. These are man-made sharpening surfaces and they come in colors. Black is X-coarse, blue is medium coarse, red is fine and green is extra fine. I then use a ceramic stone to put the finishing edge on the blade.

**How to Whittle the Whimsies of Yesterday**

A knife blade that has been shaped on the X-coarse stone and sharpened on the medium coarse stone will, in all likelihood, never have to be used on these two stones again unless the point is broken. A ceramic stone is all I use to keep the blade sharp.

In all the years I have sharpened knives, I never read in a book how to sharpen a knife, so when I began writing this section of the book, I read a few articles on the subject and found, for the most part, that I had been doing it the right way.

The circular motion and the 25 degree angle are very common methods.

Fig. #24 is a pink ceramic stone. Using the circular motion at 25 degree angle about 12 rotations like shown, and then turn the blade over and reverse the rotation until the blade is sharp. Some methods I use were never mentioned in any books. I have always stomped my own snakes, so to speak. Where some people use oil or water for a lubricant, I use saliva.

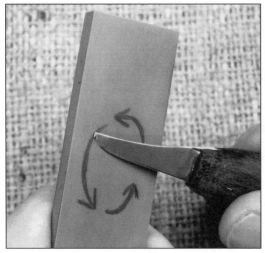

Fig. #24

Fig. #25

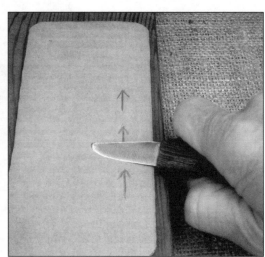

Fig. #26

How to Whittle the Whimsies of Yesterday

It works as well as water and I always have it with me. I simply moisten my finger with my tongue and apply it to the stone.

Most knife sharpeners use leather or wood for a hone. They work fine and I have used them for years, but the cardboard works better to put the shaving edge on and faster than the leather or wood. In Figs. #25 and 26 I show how I hone on cardboard with a rocking motion with the blade facing away from me. Slide the blade as the arrows show, holding the knife at the 25 degree angle. Repeat this about 12 times, then turn the knife over and repeat in the opposite direction as shown in Fig. #26. When using a hone, drag the blade only in one direction, never making the oval motion and the hone needs no lubricant. In Fig. #27 are the sharpening stones. The top one is a medium coarse diamond stone, the center is a fine coarse diamond stone, the bottom one is a pink ceramic stone and the small white one is ceramic.

The white one has a round edge and a V-shaped edge. The round edge is used to sharpen the inside curve of the gouge and the V-shaped edge is used to sharpen the V-shaped parting tool.

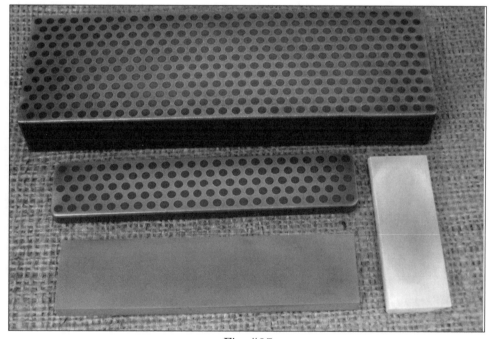

*Fig. #27*

This section deals with sharpening the gouge. Some people sharpen the gouge on the outside of the curve.

I prefer to sharpen the inside as I am doing in Fig. #28, with a curved surface that fits the inside curve of the gouge. This shape of stone is called a Slip stone. It has a long tapered edge. Use the area that best fits your gouge and rub back and forth at a 15 degree angle, being careful not to use too wide a surface as this will wear away the edge of your gouge. I use a hard wood dowel rod coated with jeweler's rouge for the inside hone. Fig. #29 is a piece of cardboard that I use to hone the outside edge. Using back and forth strokes as the arrows show and using a rolling motion so that the entire outer edge makes contact with the cardboard, or hone, if you prefer.

While I have been talking about the gouge, the epoxy has cured around our knife and handle in Fig. #30 and while you were not looking, I shaped the handle to fit my hand with the sanding wheel in my rotary tool. Always use a single blade knife to put in a wooden handle.

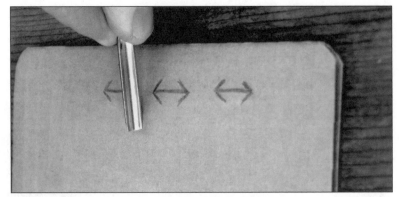
Fig #29

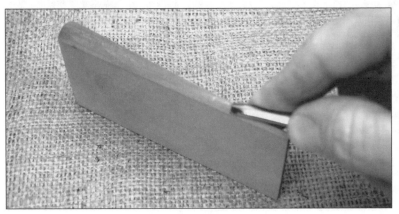
Fig. #28

Fig. #30

**How to Whittle the Whimsies of Yesterday**

# Special Tools for Special Grooves

When I started whittling chains, I never dreamed that I would some day make something that I would call a screwdriver knife. These tools will be used to make the straight-in cuts required in chain whittling and are only sharp on the round tip. (see the arrows in Fig.#33)

Fig. #31 is a 1¼" diameter piece of hard wood that is 1½" long. I have drilled a ³/₁₆" hole in the center then cut a 3½" length section off of a ³/₁₆" screwdriver. Note that I roughened up the end that is encased in the wood handle so that the epoxy will grab and hold it better.

In Fig. #32 the screwdriver has been epoxied in the handle so now you shape it to fit your palm before sharpening the tip. Fig. #33 shows the push tool which is similar to the gouge. Sharpen and shape the tip to a round shape as the photo shows. Use the extra coarse whetstone to shape the tip and the medium stone to sharpen it.

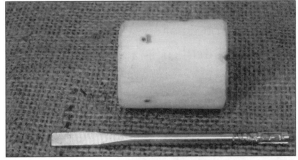

*Fig. #31*

*Fig. #32*

*Fig. #33*

Shaping the tip with the extra coarse stone will only take a few minutes.

Fig. #34 is a ⅛" screwdriver knife that can be made very easy. Don't run down to the wood and knife store and ask for a screwdriver knife, they make think you are a country bumpkin. The closest thing to a screwdriver knife will be a skew.

Fig. #35 is the hand drill. It is a very handy little tool that we will use on the wooden chains. I had been whittling the chains for years until one day it dawned on me that a small drill bit would make the chain links so much simpler. Some hobby stores have these hand drills but this one came from a welding supply store. It is the kind that some welders use to clean their acetylene torches. Some welders use a different kind so you may want to take this picture with you. We will learn how the drill will help us in the chapter on the basic wooden chain.

Fig. #36 is a little home-made knife shown in actual size. Of all of my small blade knives, it is one of my favorites and the blade is 1" long.

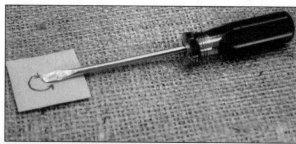

*Fig. #34*

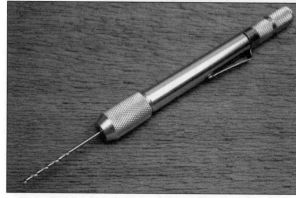

*Fig. #35*

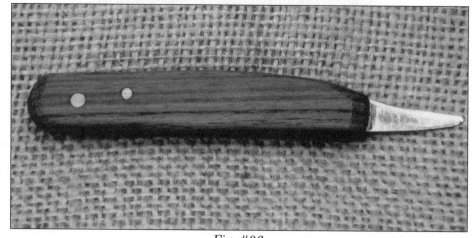

*Fig. #36*

**How to Whittle the Whimsies of Yesterday**

The knives shown on this page are actual size and all are home-made with blades sandwiched between the wooden handles. They are all used for chain whittling.

In Fig. #37, the top knife has a blade that is only ½" long and ³/₃₂" wide. I use it when whittling the very small chains. The second knife has a very sharp pointed blade of just over 1" long and it is used in the chain link separations.

In Fig. #38, the upper knife has a medium rounded point that is 1 ⅛" long. If I only had one knife to whittle with it would be one with a blade like this one. It is used in almost all the whittling projects. Note how I have shaped the handle for a perfect fit for my hand. The lower knife has a ⅝" blade. It is a little bigger than the top knife in Fig. #37 and with the five knifes you can whittle just about any project.

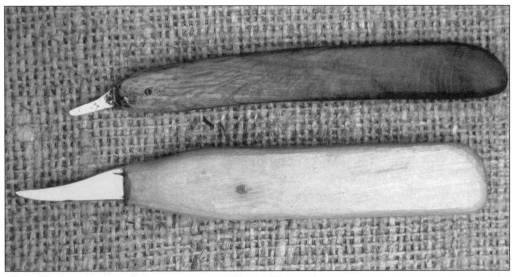

*Fig. #37*

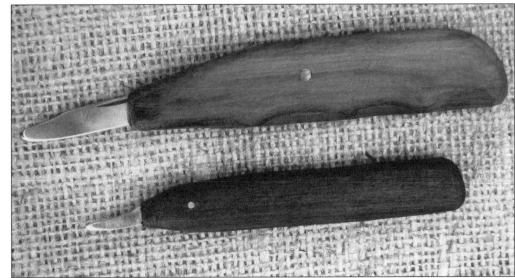

*Fig. #38*

The knives most used in this book, starting from bottom left. #1 small blade knife for small chains, #2 sharp pointed blade knife used to enlarge the X holes, #3 old round pointed knife used to whittle the balls round in the cage, #4 is my first home-made knife and the blade has worn down to half its original size and it is now in retirement, #5 is the big round bladed knife that I show how to make in Figs. #12-16, #6 is the small knife shown in Fig. #36, #7 is another old favorite, #8 is a Case Peanut in a see through handle with the blade shortened and re-shaped for whittling, and #9 is the last and least tiny little blade knife.

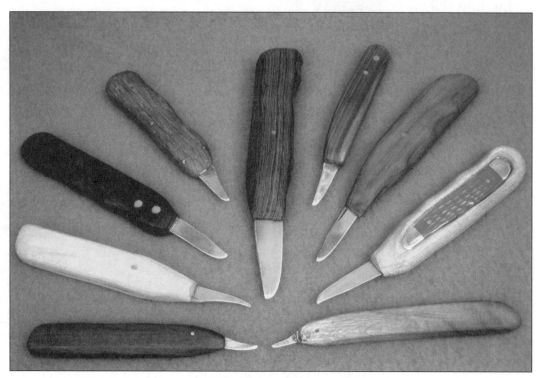

*My knife collection*

How to Whittle the Whimsies of Yesterday

Shown here are the Special Tools for Special Grooves

From left to right #1 is a store bought skew, #2 is a screwdriver knife, #3 is my first screwdriver knife in which the blade came loose and I wrapped it with a string and then epoxied it as I wrapped it (this is what you would call a poor boy's screwdriver knife), #4 is a ⅛" screwdriver knife, #5 is a small saw, #6 is a hand drill, #7 is a 3MM #5 gouge and #6 is a ³⁄₁₆" gouge. These are all the special tools for special grooves and I would be lost without them and the knives.

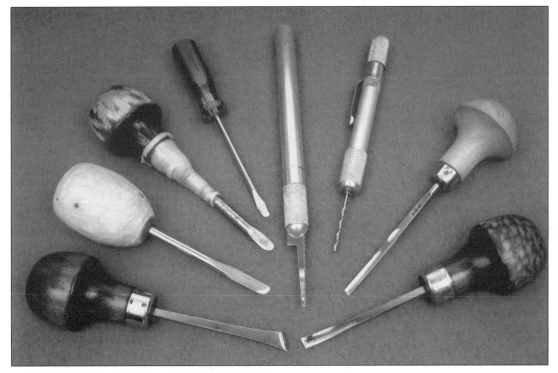

*Tools for Special Grooves*

# The Pencil

The Pencil is a simple project to get you familiar with your knife, wood and thumbguard. This whittling project can be done with a common pocket knife without a lock blade because all the cuts will be made like I am doing here, pulling the knife toward your thumb. You will want to protect your thumb from the sharp blade, though.

The thumbguard shown is homemade from a discarded tongue from an old leather shoe. I cut two holes in it and tied it in place with a leather cord. This will get you by until you can buy one. Thumbguards are very inexpensive but well worth it and you can leave the Band-Aids in the medicine cabinet.

As I was saying awhile ago, this project can be whittled with a common or regular pocket knife but not so with some of the projects in this book.

A folding knife is not made to push and force the blade into the wood mainly because it will fold over. When this happens, you will most likely be left with an injury that could have been avoided. If you can af-

ford it, run down to the woodcarver's store and invest in a thumbguard, safety glove and a knife with a locking blade. It will be the best investment you can make for your hands. Also, you might pick up a whetstone to sharpen your knife and a hone to put the finishing edge on the blade.

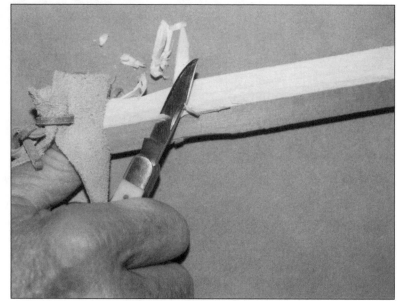

*My homemade thumbguard*

**How to Whittle the Whimsies of Yesterday**

The wood used to make The Pencil is a piece of white Pine ¾" square and 10" long. Whittle the wood to a rough point to resemble a pencil and then start whittling the square piece of wood into a round shape.

Here I am whittling the lead or the point, bringing it down to the final shape that will be our 10" long Pencil. Notice in the photo how much it resembles the lead on a real pencil! From this point, start rounding the square edges of the pencil. This is a prime example of the direction that the grain of the wood runs. You may have to whittle in the opposite direction on the other side of the wood.

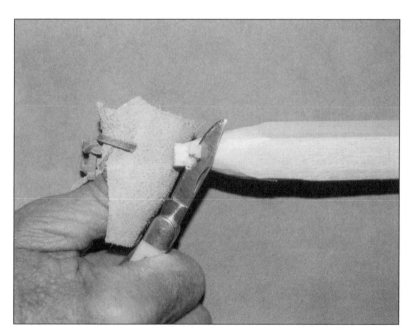
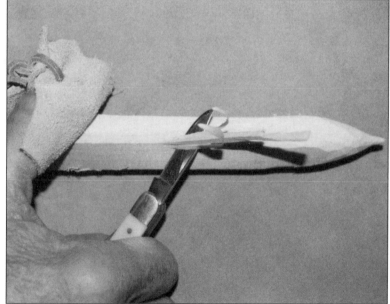

You will soon learn in which way to whittle the grain of the wood. This is one of the first and most basic things any whittler will have to master, that is, which way to do the cutting in relation to the wood grain. These are the four things used to make the "Look like" wooden pencil: a thumbguard, knife, a piece of soft wood and a felt-tip marker to paint the "lead" of the pencil. If you wanted to go a step farther, you could color the pencil yellow or any color of your choice and even paint an eraser on the other end.

How to Whittle the Whimsies of Yesterday

# The Heart

The heart they say is a fragile thing, but it is easy to whittle just the same. The one I do here is whittled out of a scrap piece of Aspen wood ¾" inch thick. Use any kind of soft wood for this project. It is shown here in actual size, so use it for a pattern to draw your heart. Make sure the grain runs up and down. You can see the darker grain on the left side.

Start carving like I have done in the photo on the following page, staying ¼" inch away from the lines all the way around. When finished, the heart will appear larger than the lines you have drawn, and have a fuller and rounder shape on the edges than if it had been sawed or cut straight down.

Notice on the lower right-hand side, the shape we are trying to achieve. Where the knife is, I am cutting with the grain. On the top and bottom, I am cutting across the grain, which is a bit harder. This is our first project in cutting across the grain and this heart was the best project I could think of for teaching that.

When you get your heart looking like the lower right hand side all the way around, then you can begin to take smaller cuts toward the lines and soon you will have your heart looking like this one. I started whittling at the top and around the right hand side and now I have started at the top whittling my way down the left side.

When you get this side rounded off like the right side, your heart will be complete, unless you want to go around the heart and whittle all the rough whittle marks a lot smoother. I like to leave the edges with the rounded effect. You can always spend another evening by the fire making it as smooth as you like. I really like the rough-hewn look like it came from a whittling session of days gone by.

# The Doughnut

Shown in actual size is the pattern for the doughnut. The gouge shown here is a ³/₁₆" #7. The #7 refers to the curve of the blade and ³/₁₆" is the width of the blade. The gouge is shown in actual size, and is a tool used for cutting below the surface, such as carving the hole through the doughnut. Using this pattern, draw your circles on any soft ¾"-1" thick piece of wood.

In Fig. #2, I started cutting the hole for the doughnut. Cutting the hole first is safer since you have a larger surface to hold on to.

When using the gouge I recommend wearing a safety glove on the hand holding the work piece. This will apply to all projects in this book. A safer way than holding the block in your hand is to lay the work piece on a non-slip surface such as

*Fig. #1*

leather that is tacked to your workbench. Chamois skin works well for this also. Keeping the gouge sharp is important for making good, clean cuts. A slip stone is used for sharpening the gouge. It is a whetstone with a round, tapered edge to fit the curved inside blade of the gouge. As I am doing in Fig. #2, cut all the way around the lines about ⅛" deep and remove the wood to this depth by prying it out of the hole. You can then proceed to cut all the way around again, repeating the prying and cutting process until you start to break through the wood. At this point, turn the wood over and work from the other side until the hole is completed. The inside of the hole will be rough, so use your knife to smooth and round out the hole.

When the hole is to your satisfaction, you are ready for the next step. The dotted lines will be the actual size of the doughnut. From the dotted lines to the solid line will be the rounded edge of the dough-nut.

You can saw or whittle the block down to the size of the dotted lines. I used a jigsaw to obtain the shape shown here in Fig. #4. Then with an ordinary pocket knife I have started whittling from the dotted lines to the solid line, rounding the edge, working all the way around the work piece. When you are whittling with the grain, you will have to take smaller cuts to keep from splitting off a large chunk of wood which could badly disfigure your doughnut.

As I have mentioned above the doughnut can be

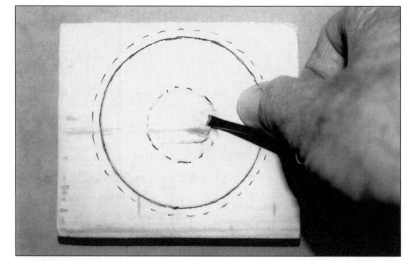
*Fig. #2*

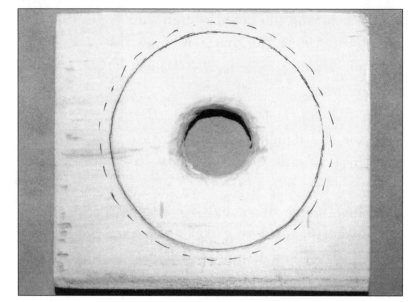
*Fig. #3*

**How to Whittle the Whimsies of Yesterday**

whittled with a folding blade pocket knife, but for the straight in cuts, required in most projects in the book, a fixed blade knife will be a must, as a folding blade will give you a bad cut.

Unlike the Heart, the doughnut should be fairly smooth. You will notice I have made the doughnut slightly oval shaped. I doubt if you have ever seen a perfectly-shaped bit of dough come out of the oven. Now spend an evening or two making your doughnut look good enough to eat.

When whittling, I get completely lost in contentment, and find that I have left all the worries of the world far, far away. For me whittling is truly a cure for stress. . . . Oh, I just whittled right through a daydream, and the doughnut is finished, and it looks like it came right out of the oven and is ready to eat. Don't try and take a bite, you might lose some teeth. If you aren't going to let anyone handle it, you can try and make it look real by applying some clear drying glue on it and sprinkle some white glitter or maybe some bright colored beads to resemble sugar sprinkles and decorations.

And now Matey, you will be chief cook and bottle washer!

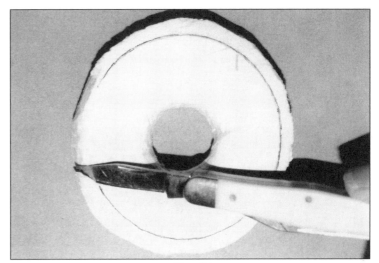
Fig. #4

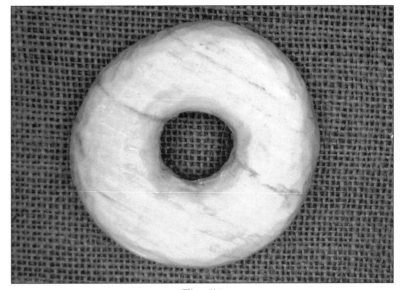
Fig. #5

**How to Whittle the Whimsies of Yesterday**

# The Airplane Propeller

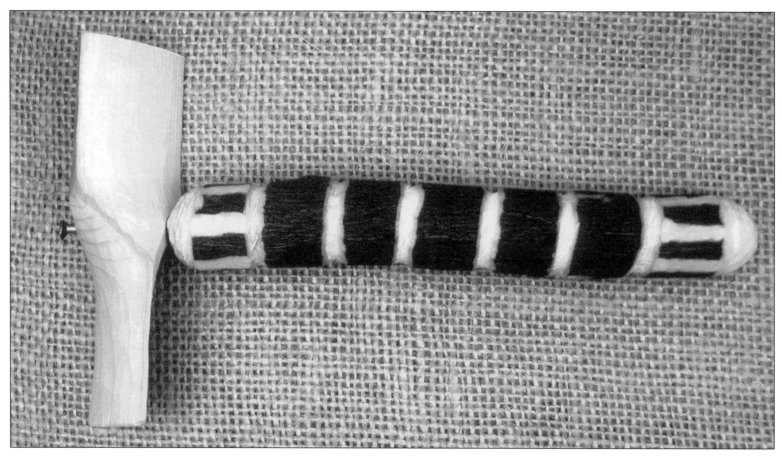

*Propeller shown actual size*

How to Whittle the Whimsies of Yesterday

## Tools you will need
## (to make the Airplane Propeller)

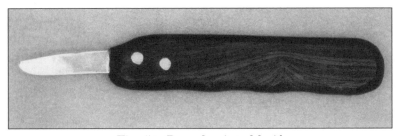

*Fig. #1. Round pointed knife*

*Fig. #2. Drill*

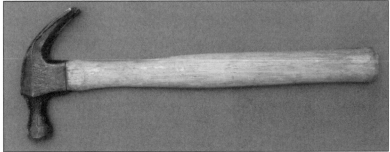

*Fig. #3. Hammer*

These are the tools you will need for this project: A sharp knife, a folding pocket knife will work. Later on in the book you will need a locking blade knife. The knife shown here is one of my homemade knives. I took the blade from an old pocketknife and sandwiched it between two pieces of wood, riveted and epoxyed it together. The blade is 1¼" long and rounded on the point. Most of your store-bought knives will have a sharp pointed blade on them which won't work for the projects we will be doing. You will also need a drill and some small drill bits so you can drill a hole through the propeller. If you don't have a drill like this one, you might want to buy a little hand drill from a hobby store which will be a lot less expensive. You will also need a hammer to drive the nail into the handle. The one shown here is half size. You might have one around the house already.

To make the airplane propeller, these are the three parts you will need: A round piece of wood for the handle, like a small branch off a mesquite tree that is 7½" long. (Later, I will cut this down to about 6" long and whittle some rings into it to make it look better and kind of like the ones I made some fifty-odd years ago.) A dowell rod can be used in place of the mesquite branch.

You will need a nail that is 1³/₄" long as it has to go through the 1" square block of the propeller and into the handle to hold it firm. You will need a 1" square block that is 4" long. The one I use here is white Pine but you can use any kind of wood for this.

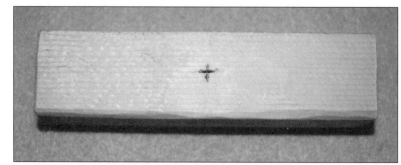

Fig. #5. 1" × 4" square block

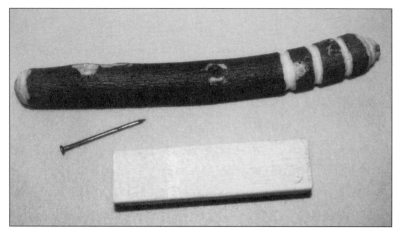

*Fig. #4. Parts for the Airplane Propeller*

Shown here is the 4"×1" square block of wood used to make the propeller. Measure very carefully to find the center of the block and mark it as I have done here with an +. Now before drilling the hole in this piece of wood, use a scrap piece of wood to test drill a hole for the nail. Keep drilling holes until you have it where the nail will slide through without binding. This is the spindle for the propeller.

After you have found the right size bit to drill the hole in the block you are going to use for the propeller, drill through the block as straight as possible. A drill press will drill this much straighter than you can doing it by hand but one of my friends has a saying that he uses quite often, "A man's gotta do what a man's gotta do." When I was a kid making these toys I didn't have a drill or a drill press! I just drilled a hole with my pocket knife. Needless to say, it would wobble in the wind, but heck it turned and back then that was all that mattered to me.

*Fig. #6. Drilling a hole through the block*

**How to Whittle the Whimsies of Yesterday**

In Fig. #7 below, the hole has been drilled and I have put the nail through to make sure it will go without binding. I then took it out so I could start the whittling. As I have shown here, begin even with the hole, whittling and rotating, whittling and rotating shaping all the corners down together. When you get the block looking more like a propeller than a block, you can start whittling back past the hole. Take a look at the next page to get an idea of where to whittle.

I have taken the shape of the propeller back ½" past the hole. Whittle slowly now, rotating and shaping with every stroke of the knife. Now the block is taking the shape of the propeller. Every now and then, put the nail through the hole and give the propeller a spin. The heavy side will stop on the bottom. Trim on the heavy side until it no longer stops on the bottom. You will have to do this until you get it ready to attach to the wooden handle. If it is not balanced, it will vibrate and wear the hole at a much faster rate.

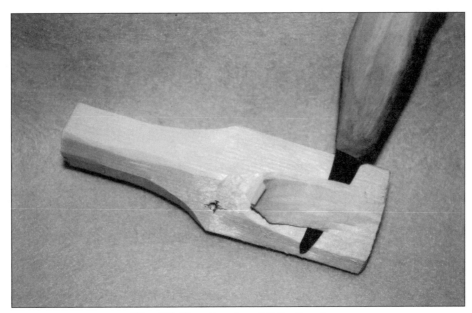

*Fig. #7. Starting to whittle the shape*

In this photo, I have shown you how much you can whittle back past the hole. The shaded part is the original part of the block that has not been whittled. You can see that there is a lot of whittling that needs to be done from Fig. #7 to Fig. #8. I have literally whittled dozens of these little toys when I was a young boy growing up in North Texas. We lived out in the country, seventeen miles from town and three miles from the nearest store where we went to buy flour and cornmeal. We didn't need to buy bread and milk since we had our own milk cow, which I milked every day, and Mother made all our bread.

With the nearest neighbor over a mile away I had loads of time to invent things to play with.

I grew up with a knife in my pocket, so it is much harder to tell you how to whittle than it is to show you. This is the reason I have so many photos for you to look at. I think you will learn more from the photos than this ol' country boy can explain it to you with words.

*Fig. #8*

**How to Whittle the Whimsies of Yesterday**

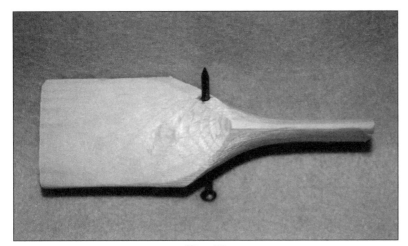

Fig. #9

The photo above is the finished propeller that is ready to nail onto the handle. It is wider than the 1" square block we started with and this is because we whittled it into a 45 degree angle, making it the width of the blade we see here 1¼" wide. The edge of the blade we see on the right hand side is a corner of the block as are the other three edges. So you can see why we drilled the hole for the nail before we started whittling, as it would be hard to get the hole through at the right angle afterwards.

The next photo shows that the blade is ¼" wide, however the thinner you can make it, the better it will turn in the wind.

After you have whittled a few of these propellers out of Pine, you can move up to a harder wood such as Oak or Ash, which will be a lot harder to whittle but will last longer. The hole in the softer wood will wear out much faster than the harder wood.

The ones I made when I was a kid were out of Mesquite wood, which is almost as hard as Oak and very plentiful in the part of the country where I grew up. You may live in a part of the world where Mesquite is not available, so just use whatever Mother Nature has provided and your toys will be unique. I am sure your kids and grandkids will enjoy them very much.

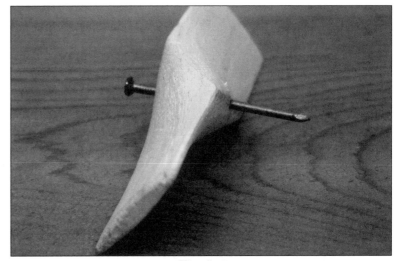

Fig. #10

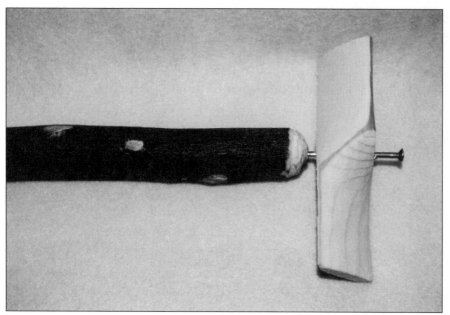

*Fig. #11*

propeller. Now you are ready for a test flight of your new toy. If the wind is not blowing strong enough, hold it in front of a fan, and watch your little creation come to life in your hand.

If your maiden flight is successful, you can now do some decorative whittling on the handle (like the photo at the start of this chapter.) If you daydream like I do while you whittle, you might come up with a one-of-a-kind that will go down in history. Speaking of history, always remember to sign and date your masterpieces because someday, someone will want to know who made it and when.

When you get your propeller looking like the one in this photo, you are ready to nail it to the handle, as shown. It will help if you pre-drill a hole in the handle, where the nail is to go, just about ⅛" deep. This will keep the handle from splitting and ensure that you get the nail in the right place. When driving the nail, set the bottom end on a solid surface, but be careful not to drive it too far. Leave it about ⅛" from the propeller. You can always drive it a little more, but it sure is hard to pull it out without damaging the

How to Whittle the Whimsies of Yesterday

Oh, the wooden chain, what a mystical thing.
It stretches our imagination and toys with our brain.
The old-timers whittled it on cold, winter days
By the potbelly stove, just to while the time away.
It takes a good evening to whittle a link on a chain,
And each link they whittled was one day closer to spring.
A good ole girl she must have been
Sweeping out all those chips and putting up with
A chain whittling man.

*Jack D. Jackson*

How to Whittle the Whimsies of Yesterday

# The Basic Chain

The chain is the foundation for the whimsy whittler. That is why I have gone into great detail along with seventy pictures to help you understand the mechanics of the wooden chain. If one picture is worth a thousand words, you should be able to whittle it by looking at the photos. The basic chain is whittled in white pine. The block is 1½" square and 13" long. You can buy this size wherever lumber is sold. They call it a 2"×2", but its actual measurement is 1½" square. This is because it has been planed down from 2"×2" to make it smooth. This makes a good wood for practice whittling as an 8' piece cost about the same as a loaf of bread. Our chain will be 9" long, with a half link attaching the chain to the square block, in which we can carve

*Photo #1*

something when our chain is finished. The 9" chain will have five links that are $2\frac{5}{8}$" long, and one link only $1\frac{3}{4}$" long. We will lay out the chain in steps, starting with Photo #2.

**Step One**: Number all four sides of the block, 3" from the end in big, black numbers as in these two photos. Put the numbers in a left to right rotation. Be sure Sides #1 and #3 are on opposite sides, and Sides #2 and #4 are on opposite sides. This is very critical as each opposing side will be drawn and whittled in such a way as to meet each other in the center of the block.

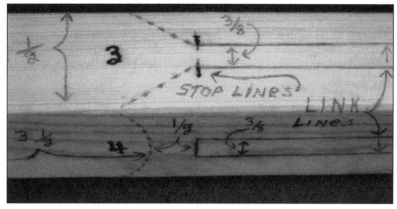

*Photo #3. View of Side #3 and Side #4*

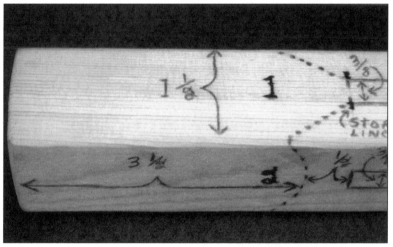

*Photo #2. View of Side #1 and Side #2*

**Step Two**: Measure 3½" from the end of the block and put a dot, as on Sides #2 and #4. Make a curved, dotted line back ⅜" to the corner of the block, as on Sides #2 and #4.

**Step Three**: From the dotted line on Sides #2 and #4, measure ½" to the right and mark the end of the link lines.

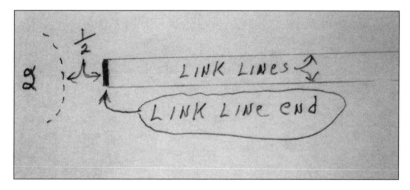

**Step Four**: You are now ready to draw the link lines on Sides #2 and #4. Starting at the end of the link line marks, draw the link lines ⅜" wide to the end of the block, center them up as close as you can.

Photo #4 shows the 13" block with all four sides drawn and ready for the knife. Photo #5 shows the far end of the block with the sides numbered. Note how the link lines form an + on the end of the block. The link lines must be centered to form the cross.

**Step Five**: On Sides #1 and #4, draw the little lines I call stop lines. These lines should be lined up with the end of the link lines on Sides #2 and #4. (See Photo #2.)

From the stop lines on Sides #1 and #3, dot a line back to intersect with the curved dotted lines on Sides #2 and #4. Shown on Side #1.

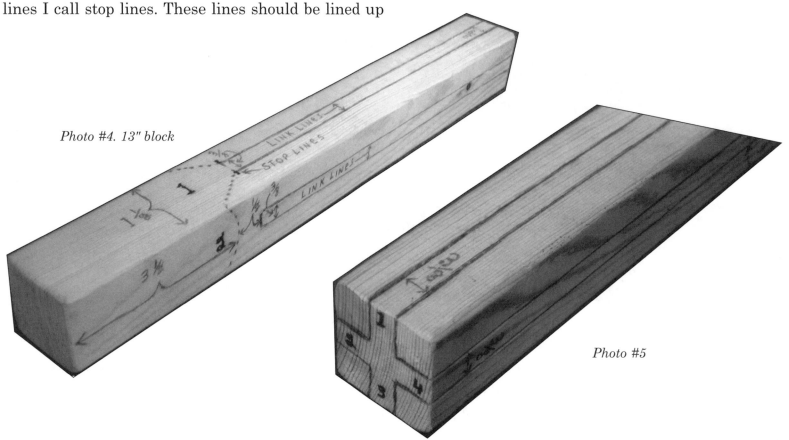

*Photo #4. 13" block*

*Photo #5*

**How to Whittle the Whimsies of Yesterday**

**Step Six**: Starting at the stop lines on Sides #1 and #3, draw in the link lines, making them form a cross on the end of the block, as on the end view here. I pondered for days on a name for the little stop lines: start of the chain lines—end of the chain lines—two little stop signs—that's it. STOP LINES, not stop signs. Decisions, decisions!

With the link lines drawn, the stop lines in place, the sides numbered and the dotted lines dotted, we are ready to get started doing the straight-in cuts with the screwdriver knife or a skew if it is store bought.

**Step Seven**: In photo #6, Side #1 with the screwdriver knife, I have started the straight-in cuts, placing the block on a non-slip surface. Make the straight-in cuts about ¼" deep, following the link lines toward the stop lines. Stop the cut ¼" from the stop lines as shown here in Photo #7. Cut both lines on Side #1, from the cross to within ¼" of the stop lines. Now turn to Side #3 and repeat the cut.

**Step Eight**: Cut the link lines on Sides #2 and #4 starting at the cross.

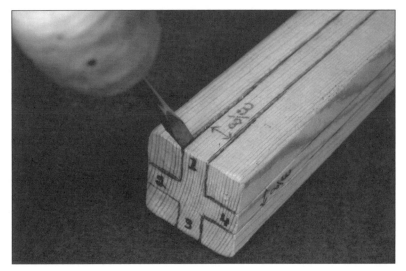

*Photo #6*

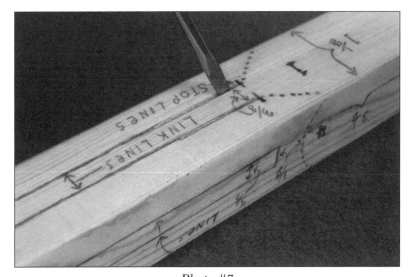

*Photo #7*

*Photo #8*

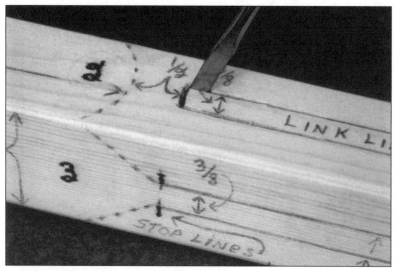

*Photo #9*

As in Photo #8, follow the link line up to the end of the link as in Photo #9.

In Photo #10, I am making the cross grain end of the link cut (this is done only on Sides #2 and #4.) Now after making the end cut, follow the link line back down this side of the line to the cross.

Now turn to Side #4 and repeat this cut. When all four sides are cut ¼" deep, the time for whittling away some of our unwanted wood has finally arrived, thank goodness. I would rather whittle than draw lines and dots.

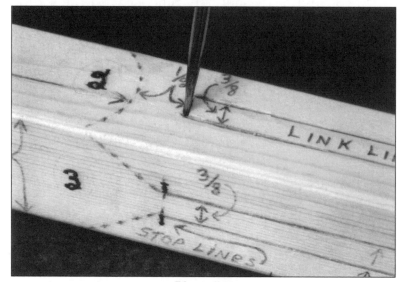

*Photo #10*

**How to Whittle the Whimsies of Yesterday**

*Photo #11*

*Photo #12*

**Step Nine**: All of the straight-in cuts have been made. I have shaded the unwanted wood that needs to be whittled away around the cross. We will have to do this all the way along the link lines leaving only the cross when we have finished this step.

In Photo #12, I am deepening the straight-in cuts that we made only ¼" deep. On the first straight-in cut, the ³⁄₁₆ gouge works well to remove the unwanted wood. Be sure to wear the safety glove on the hand that is holding the work piece and work on a non-slip surface. The gouge is notorious for a bad puncture wound. Work safe and don't spill that good, red blood.

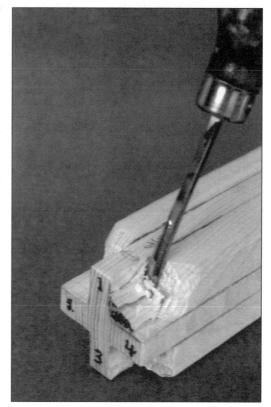

*Photo #13*

*Photo #14*

**Step Ten**: With the unwanted wood removed the entire length of the link lines, we now have link bars which stop at the stop lines on Sides #1 and #3 and at the end of the link marks on Sides #2 and #4.

In Photo #15, I have started at the dotted lines on Sides #2 and #4, removing the wood from the curved dotted lines to the end of the link bar.

Photo #16 shows what your work piece should look like when this step is done. You can use a knife or a gouge for this work, but be careful not to split the end of the link bars.

*Photo #15*

*Photo #16*

**How to Whittle the Whimsies of Yesterday**

**Step Eleven**: Laying out the chain, beginning with the half link or joining link. The half link joins the square block to the chain. Shown here on Side #2 is the layout for the half link. The shaded area encircles the end of the link bar. The shaded oval circle is 1" long (which will be the hole) and ¾" wide and wraps around the link bar ¾" The hole for the half link will be cut from Side #2 through to Side #4. The arrows pointing to the overlap area (the darker area) is where the separation cuts will be made to separate the links.

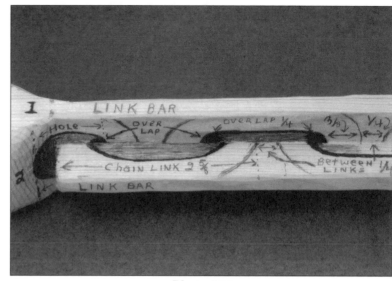

*Photo #18*

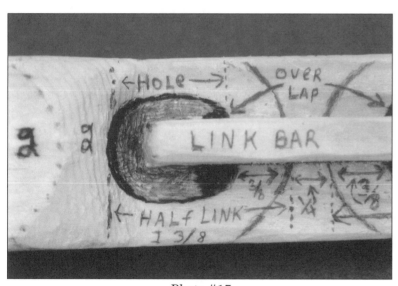

*Photo #17*

The half link is 1⅜" long. The link will be approximately ⅜" in diameter, as will all the links.

Photo #18 shows an angle view to better show the overlap separation points which are ¼", for the basic chain which we are doing here. When each separation cut is made, the chain will get ¼" longer. This means our 9" chain could grow over 1" longer when finished.

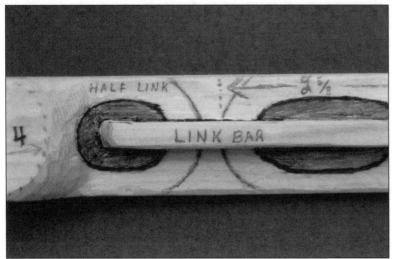

*Photo #19*

between Side #1 and #2. The shaded areas are where we will remove the unwanted wood to form the inside holes for the chain links.

The round end of the links are with the grain, therefore they are much easier to split or break than the long side, so let's leave the round ends of the links a bit larger in diameter than the long sides of the links.

The half link in Photo #19 shows Side #4 which is identical to the opposite Side #2. When we start the cut on Side #2, it will come out on Side #4, leaving the link bar in place (a hole around the link bar.)

Photo #20 is an angle view between Side #3 and #4. It is drawn exactly like the view in Photo #18,

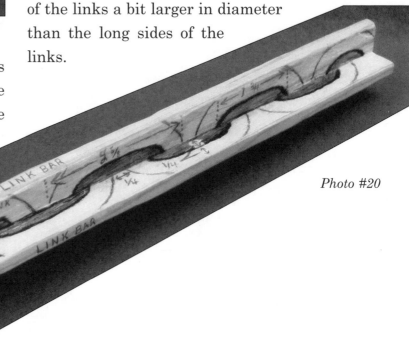

*Photo #20*

**How to Whittle the Whimsies of Yesterday**

Shown here are Sides #1 and #3, laid out exactly the same on each side.

The large links are 2⅝" long with the shaded areas 1¾" long. The distance between the big links is ¼".

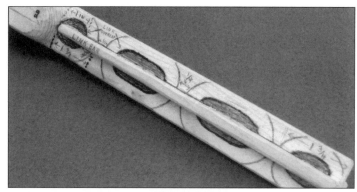

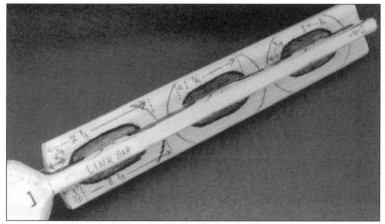

*Photo #21*

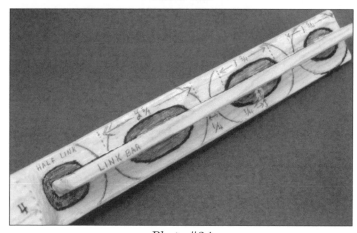

*Photo #23*

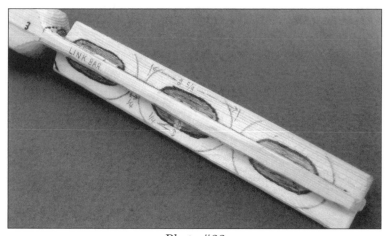

*Photo #22*

*Photo #24*

Sides #2 and #4 are drawn to be exactly like each other. The small link on the end is 1¾" in length, the shaded area is 1" long, the same size as the half link shaded area.

With all four sides drawn, we are ready to start the cut on the half link, Side #2.

**Step Twelve**: Cutting the hole for the half link, from Side #2 to Side #4.

First, make a straight-in cut around the outside and inside of the shaded area as shown in Photo #25, 26 and 27. Make the cut about ⅛" deep, being sure to go straight down around the end of the link bar, as shown in Photo #26. When you have the straight-in cut made all the way around, start removing the wood in the shaded area. In Photo #28, I am using a #3 × ⅛ palm gouge to remove the unwanted wood. When you have the wood removed ⅛" deep, make another straight-in cut around the hole and dig it out again.

*Photo #26*

*Photo #27*

*Photo #28*

*Photo #25*

How to Whittle the Whimsies of Yesterday

*Photo #29*

**Step Thirteen**: Making the second straight-in cut. In this cut I am about halfway through to Side #4. When I feel the point of the knife break through to Side #4, I then turn the work piece over and start the straight-in cuts from Side #4.

Make the straight-in cut all the way around just like we did on Side #2. Dig out the unwanted wood with the work piece on a non-slip surface. Do not hold it in your hand at this point for obvious safety reasons.

*Photo #30*

*Photo #31*

When you have the cut made from Side #2 to Side #4, the hole should look like the one here in Photo #32. There is still some cleanup work to do but it is just some minor whittling to round off the link, which we will leave until we have the link separated.

**Step Fourteen**: Learning the separation technique.

In Photo #18, the overlap shading can be seen very clearly. On this big link basic chain, we have ¼" to make the separation cut. On the smaller chains there will be less than ¹⁄₁₆" to make these same cuts. On the very small chains I use a small hand drill to make

what I call the X cuts. That is to simply drill a hole in from the four sides of the separation overlap.

I have started the X holes in Photos #33, #34, and #35.

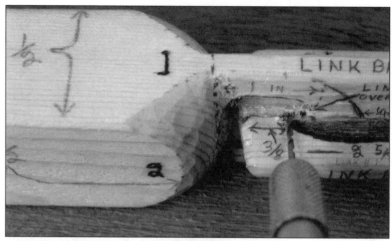

*Photo #33*

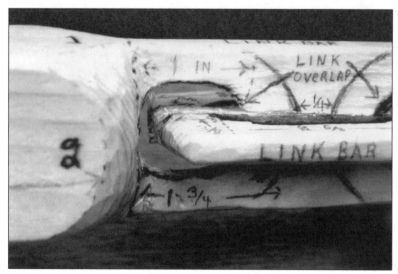

*Photo #32. The Hole*

*Photo #34*

**How to Whittle the Whimsies of Yesterday**

*Photo #35*

sides as opposed to drilling completely through it. If the angle is not right, the drill bit will come out on the side of the link, thus ruining or considerably damaging a link.

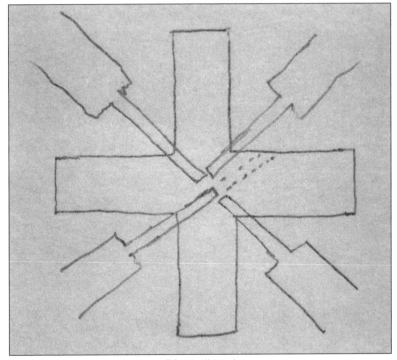

*Photo #35-A*

With the ¼" overlap we have on our big basic chain we could whittle the cut with a small gouge or a thin bladed knife, but since we are doing the big chain to learn the mechanics, we will do the X hole cuts. The idea is to remove the wood to separate the links, drilling in from all four sides as the photos and the diagram show. These little holes make it a lot easier to get a thin knife blade through to clean out the cut.

The diagram shows why we drill in from the four

We drill in from all four angles and then with a thin, sharp pointed knife, we work the blade into the X holes, enlarging them and removing the wood fibers in very small pieces. Work the knife in from all four sides until the separation hole is complete. When working with the sharp pointed knife to whittle the separation hole, you will have to hold the work piece, so WEAR THE SAFETY GLOVE!

In Photo #37, the separation hole has been roughed out. We are ready for the next phase of forming our half link. I think by now, you can see how the half link is going to look and I would bet you know what the next step will be.

*Photo #36*

*Photo #37*

**How to Whittle the Whimsies of Yesterday**

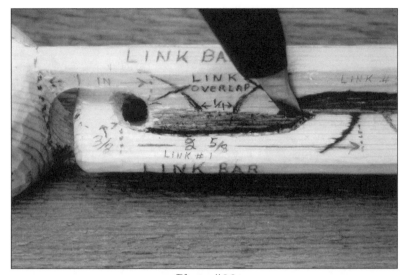

*Photo #38*

*Photo #40*

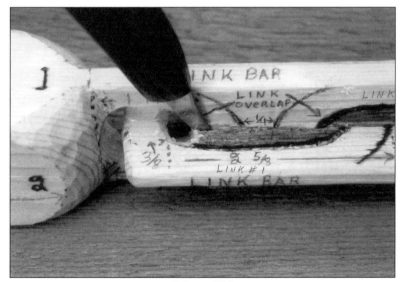

*Photo #39*

**Step Fifteen**: If you guessed it would be making the straight-in cuts around the shaded area of link #1—you are 100% right. Make the straight-in cuts as we did on the half link, making them about ⅛" deep. Go completely around the inside of the shaded area and also around the outside, as shown in these three photos. When you have the straight-in cuts done on Side #1, you are ready to whittle away some unwanted wood. Remember Side #3 is on the opposite side.

The straight-in cuts being made, I am digging away the shaded area. When you have the wood removed ⅛" deep, make the straight-in cut around the hole a second time and dig out the hole again. In Photo #42, the knife blade has poked through to Side #3, so I have turned the work piece over in Photo #43 and started making the straight-in cuts from Side #3 so as to intersect with the cut we started on Side #1.

*Photo #42*

*Photo #41*

*Photo #43*

**How to Whittle the Whimsies of Yesterday**

With the link hole cut through in Photo #44 from Side #1 to Side #3, we are ready for the next step.

**Step Sixteen**: Cutting the half link free. We will start this cut on Side #2 and Side #4, whittling on one side and then the other until our half link has been separated. Whittle, following the lines that we have drawn for the link shape. (Photos #45 and 46)

*Photo #45*

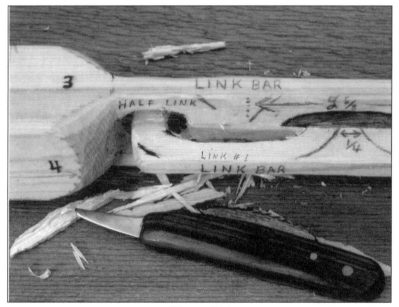

*Photo #44*

*Photo #46*

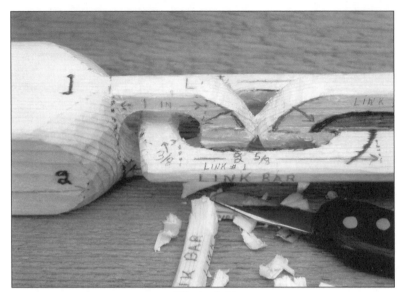

*Photo #47*

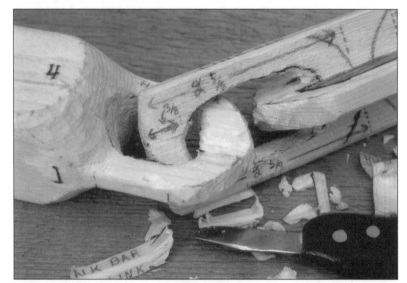

*Photo #48*

*Photo #49*

In Photo #47 the cut is almost finished. In Photo #48, the half link is free, but still needs some clean up whittling to make it look more like a link than a rough piece of wood.

This happens to be my favorite part of whimsy whittling, rounding off the corners and doing the dress up whittling. In Photo #49 we are finishing up rounding off the last corner and are now ready for the next step.

**How to Whittle the Whimsies of Yesterday**

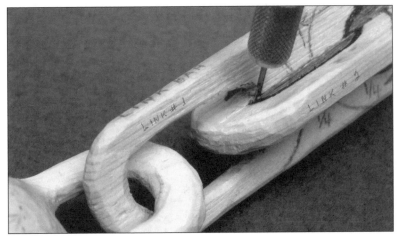

*Photo #50*

*Photo #52*

**Step Seventeen**: Making the next X hole cut as shown above. I will not dwell on the X holes or the separation cuts as they are done just like the one we did in Photos #33-37.

**Step Eighteen**: Making the straight-in cuts and cutting our way from Side #2 to Side #4 on link #2.

After the hole is cut in link #2, we now have room to make the cut to free link #1.

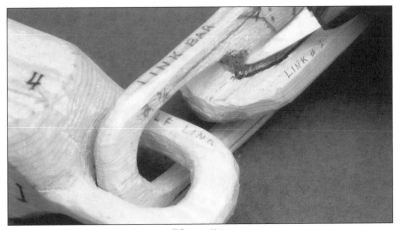

*Photo #51*

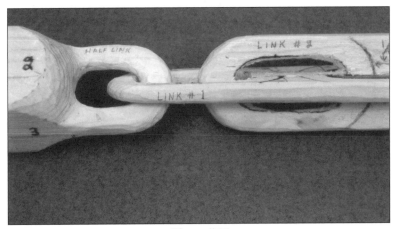

*Photo #53*

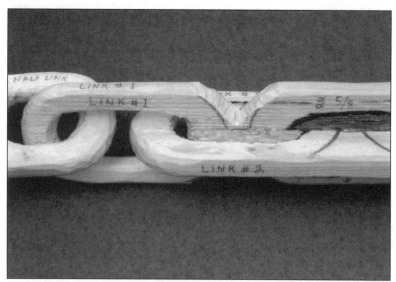

*Photo #54*

**Step Nineteen**: Cutting link #1 free. This cut is made just like the cut we made in Photos #47 and 48.

In Photo #55, link #1 has been cut free. In Photo #56, link #1 has been whittled clean. It seems to me that this chain whittling is becoming routine, and whittling friend of mine, we have just finished step nineteen.

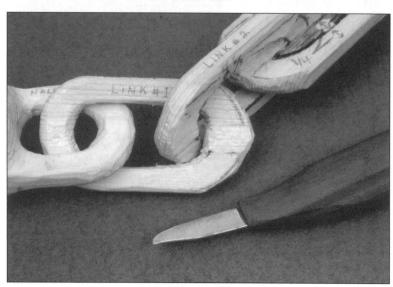

*Photo #55*

*Photo #56*

**How to Whittle the Whimsies of Yesterday**

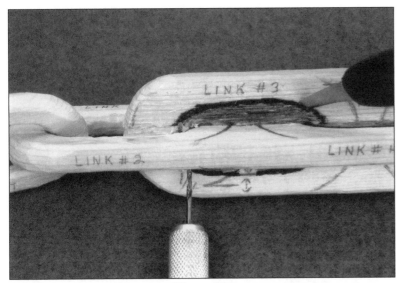
*Photo #57*

**Step Twenty**: Drill the X holes, clean out the debris, do the straight-in cuts on the link #3.

When the straight-in cuts are done, whittle through just like we did on links #1 and 2.

In Photo #58, we are ready to make the cut to set free Link #2.

Photo #59 shows Link #2 is now a part of the chain. We are now ready for Step Twenty-one, where we will do the same thing again.

*Photo #58*

*Photo #59*

*Photo #60*

**Step Twenty-one**: In Photo #60 we have a view from the end of the cross showing what we have accomplished thus far and drilling the X holes between Links #3 and #4. Photo #61 shows the debris removed from the X hole cut.

In Photo #62 I am doing the straight-in cut around the shaded area of Link #4.

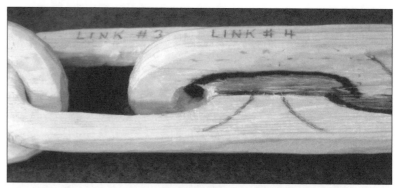

*Photo #61*

*Photo #62*

Photo #63 shows the straight-in cut has been finished around the entire shaded area of Link #4 and the unwanted wood is being removed to form Link #4.

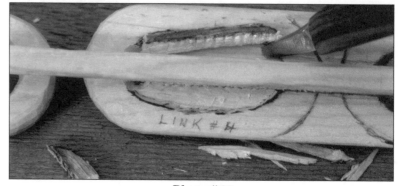

*Photo #63*

**How to Whittle the Whimsies of Yesterday**

Photo #64 shows the cut to free Link #3 is almost done. Finish this cut and do the cleanup whittling on Link #3 and you are ready for the X hole cut between Link #4 and #5.

In Photo #65, I have omitted showing the X hole cuts and the shaded area cuts which brings us to Link #6, the least and last link of our basic chain.

Link #6 will be done just like the other links except for two things. One is removing all the wood on Link #5 to the end of the link bar, as I will show you in our last step. The other is to drill the X holes on both ends of the shaded area.

*Photo #64*

*Photo #65*

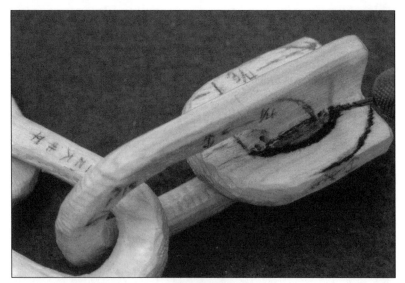

*Photo #66*

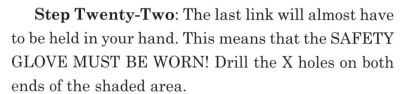

**Step Twenty-Two**: The last link will almost have to be held in your hand. This means that the SAFETY GLOVE MUST BE WORN! Drill the X holes on both ends of the shaded area.

Photo #67 shows that you need to remove the debris from inside the X holes and whittle away the remaining wood on the end of Link #5.

Photo #68 shows the straight-in cuts and then you will remove the unwanted wood in the shaded area, cutting the hole for the link.

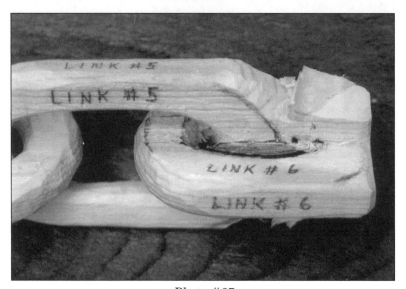

*Photo #67*

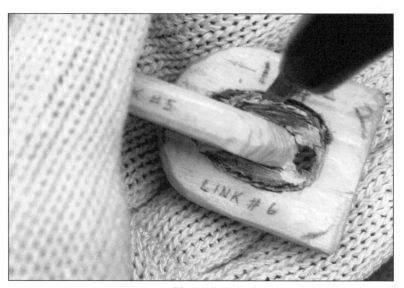

*Photo #68*

**How to Whittle the Whimsies of Yesterday**

**Step Twenty-Three:** When I first started whittling chains, it was like taking a banana from a gorilla, but now it is as easy as taking a nap on a feather pillow.

Once you have Link #6 cut free, all you will like being done is whittling the link pretty and round. I hope you have had a good time learning how the chain works, as we will be doing them smaller and smaller.

Remember I told you that our chain would grow longer as we cut our overlap separations? In the beginning, the bars of our chain were 9" long. Each time a separation cut was made, our chain grew about a ¼". Now our chain is 10⅜" long! Who said you can't stretch wood. We just did.

*Photo #69*

*Photo #70*

The chain is done but we still have a 3½" block of wood attached to it that we could make something out of.

I have an idea or two, if you have time, and we will see what we can come up with to add to our book of whimsies. Do you think we might whittle a cage with something inside that would actually protrude out the sides through the bars? Just how would we go about doing something like that?

*Photo #71*

How to Whittle the Whimsies of Yesterday

# The Football in a Cage

To lay out the cage for our Football in a Cage, start drawing the lines ½" from the end of the block. Next, draw the cage bars ¼" from the edge all the way around on all four sides as shown in Photo #1.

When all four sides are drawn in, begin the straight-in cuts as shown in Photo #2. Make these cuts ³⁄₁₆" deep all the way around. As you get to the curved top lines as in Photo #3, and the straight line cut shown in Photo #4.

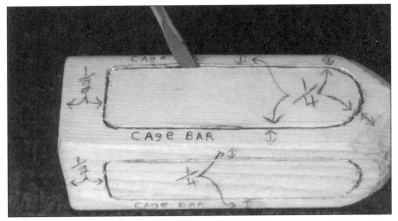

*Photo #2*

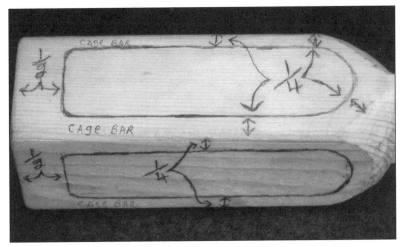

*Photo #1*

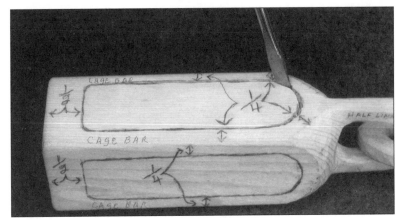

*Photo #3*

These will be cross-grain cuts and therefore much harder to cut. You might want to use a sharp pointed knife with a short blade which will penetrate the cross-grain much better. Just be sure to place the block on a non-slip surface and WEAR THE SAFETY GLOVE while making these cuts.

When all of the straight-in cuts have been made, take a ³⁄₁₆ gouge and begin removing the unwanted wood like I have shown in Photo #5.

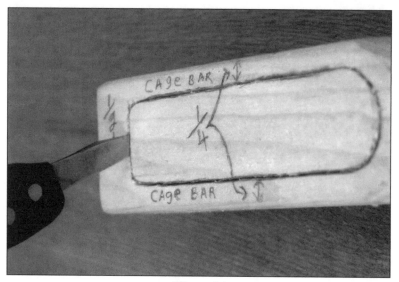

*Photo #4*

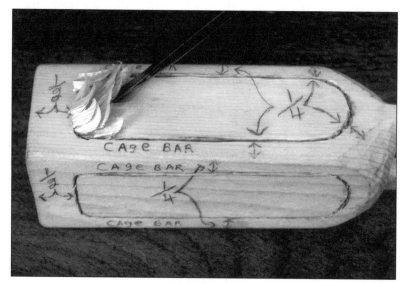

*Photo #5*

**How to Whittle the Whimsies of Yesterday**

Gouge out both ends on all four sides to the depth of the straight-in cuts. The straight-in cuts will have to be deepened on the ends. As I show in Photo #6, use the gouge to deepen the cuts now that you are below the surface. In Photo #7, I have removed the wood along the cage bars, going no deeper than the $^{3}/_{16}$" straight-in cut for now. As you deepen the end cuts, you will also have to deepen the side cuts like I show in Photo #8.

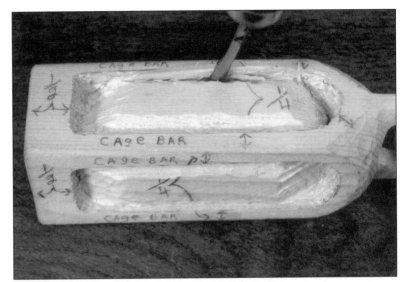

*Photo #7*

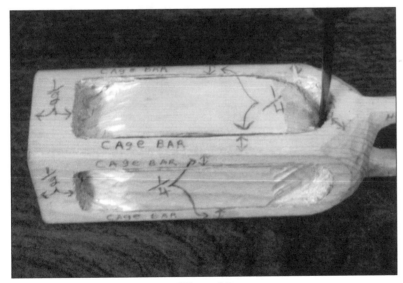

*Photo #6*

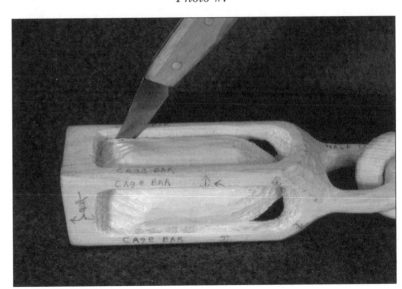

*Photo #8*

**How to Whittle the Whimsies of Yesterday**

Shape the football, but leave it attached to the cage bars where I have shaded the center stripe. In Photo #9, the ends are not yet cut free. Leave the ends and center attached as long as possible to obtain the shape of the football. Leaving these six points attached will keep the ball stable while you shape it and will also give the bars more strength while holding it.

I am shaving the inside of the bars in Photo #10, and removing the unwanted wood to shape the football.

The cage bars when finished will be sort of triangular in shape. If they were left completely square then the football would have to be much smaller.

*Photo #10*

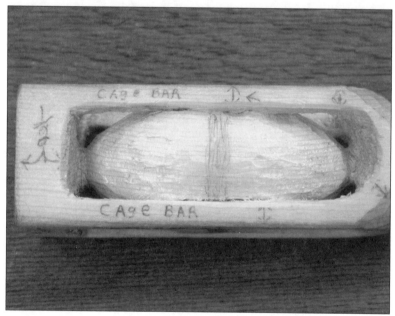

*Photo #9*

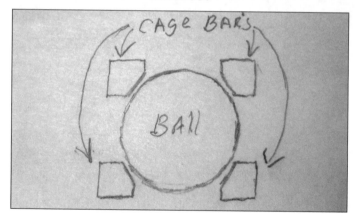

*Photo #10-A. Inside sketch of the cage bars*

**How to Whittle the Whimsies of Yesterday**

Shaving away the stripe around the football, taking only about 1/32" off and trimming the bars from inside will give us enough room to free the ball from the bars.

In Photo #12, the football is free of all four bars with only the ends of the football holding it in place. The football is free in Photo #13. The football needs trimming so that it will turn sideways in the cage.

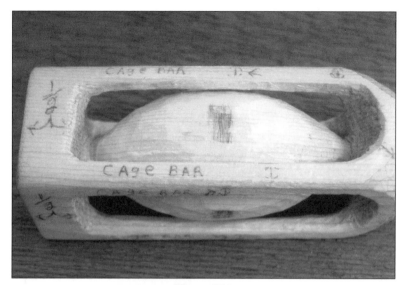

*Photo #12*

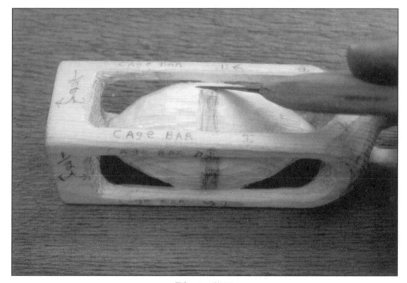

*Photo #11*

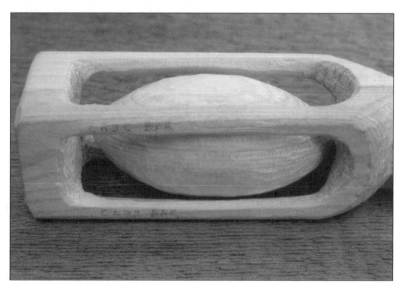

*Photo #13*

The football and chain are finished and ready for the game. From Photo #13 to Photo #14, trimming the football so that it will turn sideways in the cage will take two or three evenings of very fine whittling. The trick is to get the football to turn crossways in the cage without falling through the bars. Whittle slow, taking only fine shavings off and be patient. It can be done. The football in a cage with the chain makes a wonderful conversation piece.

*Photo #14*

**How to Whittle the Whimsies of Yesterday**

# Two Balls in a Cage

The Two Balls in a Cage will be whittled out of a piece of Bass wood that is 18" long and 1" square. This will be the beginning of the Whimsy shown on the front cover of this book. It will also consist of the Two Joining Links, the Slider, another Half-Link and the Split Chain all whittled out of one 18" long block of wood!

The Two Balls in a Cage will be much like the Football in a Cage except everything is done on a much smaller scale.

The cage bars are ³/₁₆" wide whereas the bars on the Football in a Cage were ¼" wide.

Just for practice, you may want to whittle your first Two Balls in a Cage on a shorter piece of wood before starting on the 18" block. That's what I did.

I am using my old round pointed fixed blade knife to make the straight-in cuts here but you could use the screwdriver knife instead. The Cage is 3" long from the bottom to the pointed top. Leave ³/₈" on the bottom for strength. Be sure that the bottom and top of the Cage are lined up all the way around. Remember when doing the straight-in cuts, the work piece should be placed on a non-slip surface for safety. ***Folding knives will not work on straight-in cuts!***

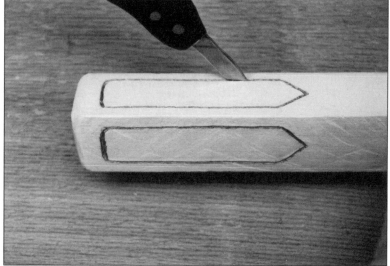

*Fig. #1*

In Fig. #1, the straight-in cuts have been made ⅛" deep along the sides. The cuts on each end of the Cage can be made deeper since all of the wood on the ends must be removed as shown in Fig. #5.

Fig. #2 shows the old round pointed knife used to whittle the Two Balls in a Cage.

Fig. #3 shows the ³⁄₁₆ #7 gouge. As I am showing here (top view only) gouge around the edges only as deep as the straight-in cuts. Leave the midsection rounded like the front view. On the left side of the front view I have gouged about halfway through the block. This will be done on both ends and all four sides. Keep in mind that the oval ball must be a full 2⅛" long and even a bit longer won't hurt. Too short though and you will only have one ball. Leaving the oval ball attached to the cage bars will make the following cuts much easier.

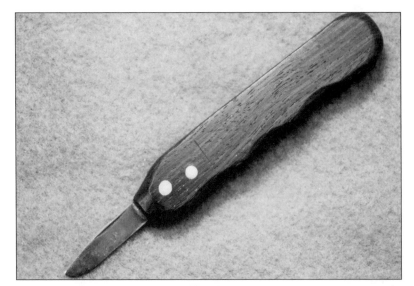

*Fig. #2*

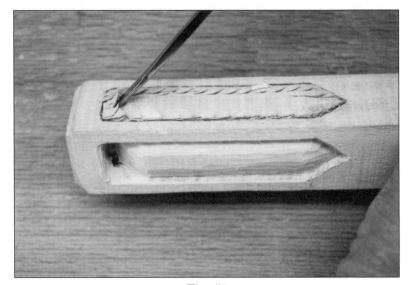

*Fig. #3*

**How to Whittle the Whimsies of Yesterday**

When making the cuts from Fig. 3 through Figs. 4 and 5, be very careful not to damage the Cage's bars. The inside of the Cage bars will be triangular in shape. (Refer back to Photo #10 in the Football in a Cage section or ahead to Fig. 8-A in this section.) In Fig. #4, the oval ball is taking shape but look ahead to Photo #7 and note that the balls are still attached to the Cage bars. The gouge will make the rough digging cuts needed to hollow out the ends.

In Fig. #5, I have used the round pointed knife to round the ends of the oval ball. I have drawn a line around the center of the oval ball and drawn arrows on each side of the solid line. The little arrows are about ⅛" long. They will come in handy in the following steps.

Fig. #4

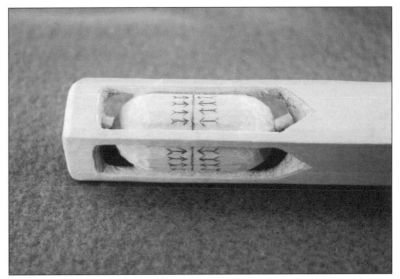

Fig. #5

The Cage is 3" long from the bottom to the pointed top. The oval ball is 2¼" long and still firmly attached to the bars, making it strong enough to do the heavy whittling in the remaining steps.

On the solid line around the oval ball make a straight-in cut ⅛" deep on the line all the way around the oval ball, as in Fig. 6.

After the cut in Fig. 6 is complete, we are ready to find out what all those little arrows are about.

As I have done in Fig. 7, with the gouge or the round pointed knife, start at the tail of the arrows and cut towards the center. Go all the way around and cut until all those little arrows are turned into chips.

(NOTE: Where the pencil is pointing, notice how much wood is still holding the balls firmly attached to the bars.)

Go around another time making the cut a little wider and a little deeper until you have it looking like the work piece in Fig. 8.

*Fig. #6*

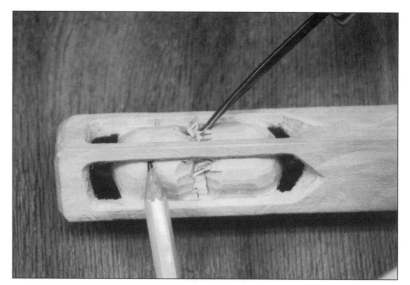
*Fig. #7*

How to Whittle the Whimsies of Yesterday

From Fig. #7 to Fig.#8, I have gouged away the little arrows and now have the oval ball cut about halfway in two. I am using the thin, sharp pointed blade to trim the inside of the Cage bars into the triangular shape needed on the inside (as shown in sketch 8-A ). The balls can be bigger when the inside of the bars are trimmed.

From Fig. #8 to the finished balls will take patience, so settle back in your easy chair with a towel in your lap to catch the shavings and spend another two or three evenings giving these little balls their freedom to roll around in the cage.

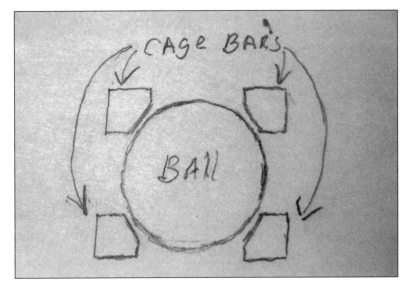

*Fig. #8-A*

*Fig. #8*

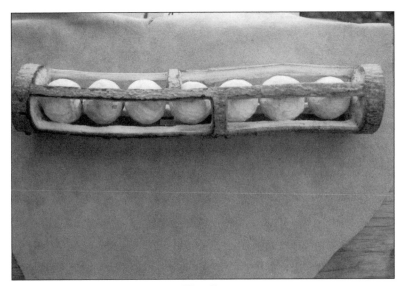

*Fig. #9*

**How to Whittle the Whimsies of Yesterday**

*Fig. #10*

The Log Full O' Balls shown in Fig. #9 is whittled out of Aspen wood. Years ago I experimented to try and see how many balls I could get in a cage but the bars were too weak for more than five or six until I began putting a dummy ball in every now and then for support. The Log Full O' Balls has only three free-rolling balls and the rest are attached at alternating places for support.

Was it worth all the time and hard, tedious work just to have two balls in a cage that serve no purpose, other than a conversation piece? They truly are a whim and look more like the moon through a telescope than actual balls. This just adds character and charm and speaks louder than words that they really were just a piece of wood a few days ago.

I have whittled a lot of balls in cages and have tried to make two just alike but because they are handmade and in wood with grain, there will never be two just alike. So when your whimsy is finished, you can say with pride, "There is not another one like this on the entire planet!" That also goes for the other projects we will whittle.

# The Joining Links

The Basic Chain had one half-link joining the Football Cage to the chain. The Joining Links will join the Two Balls in a Cage to the Slider.

When making the straight-in cuts for the Two Balls in a Cage, I used the round pointed knife but gave you a choice to use the screwdriver knife. Making the straight-in cuts for the Half-Links we encounter cross grain cuts on the bar ends and they are

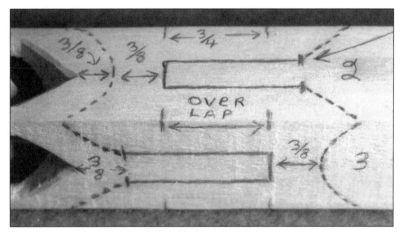

*Photo #2*

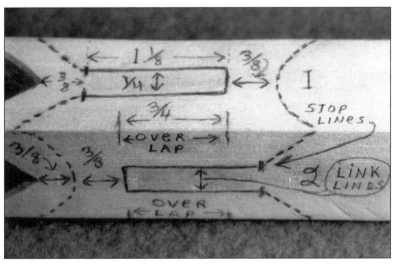

*Photo #1*

too narrow to make with the round pointed knife. I use the ⅛" screwdriver knife or the small knife shown in Fig. #36 in the Special Tools for Special Grooves Section for the narrow cross grain cuts. As with the Basic Chain, number all four sides to prevent confusion. The first four photos show you how to lay out the Joining Links and they are enlarged to show the drawings more clearly. The solid link lines are the most important but so are the stop lines. They are where we will start and stop the cuts. The dotted lines are not as important as the solid lines but will help us later on in this project. The solid lines are ¼" apart and 1⅛" long. The best place to start your drawing is on Side #2 with the curved dotted line ⅜" from the point of the Two Balls in a Cage, and then ⅜" to the end of the Link bar as shown on previous page. Side #4 will be drawn exactly the same as Side #2 and Sides #1 and #3 are drawn exactly the same. Draw Side #1 after you have drawn Side #2. On Sides #1 and #3 measure ⅜" from the point of the cage and draw the stop lines (where the pencil is pointing). Now, dot a straight line from the stop lines to intersect with the curved lines on Sides #2 and #4. I stress again that Sides #1 and #3 must be drawn exactly the same. And Sides #2 and #4 are drawn exactly the same.

In these photos you can see a line I call the overlap line. This is the distance that the links must overlap each other in order to have room to make the separation cuts. This distance is ¾.".

All these dots, lines, numbers, curves, and square turns make my head swim, but I wanted you to see all four sides in their entirety so that maybe, just maybe, you will have a little sympathy for me for dreaming up a project like this!

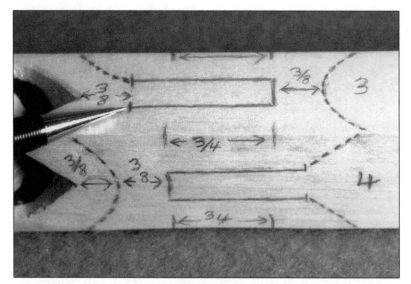

*Photo #3*

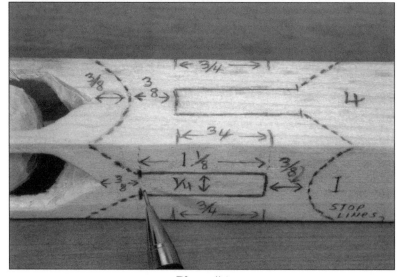

*Photo #4*

**78**

In Photo #5, the pencil points to the stop line. This is where we will start the straight-in cuts on the link lines. With a screwdriver knife or a small round pointed knife that has a stationary blade, make this straight down cut all the way around the link and back to the stop line.

Make the cut (where the blade is in the photo) only ⅛" deep. In Photo #6, I moved the screwdriver knife the width of the blade, making the cut a little deeper as I move away from the stop line. As you work your way to the end of the link you should make the cut no deeper than ¼".

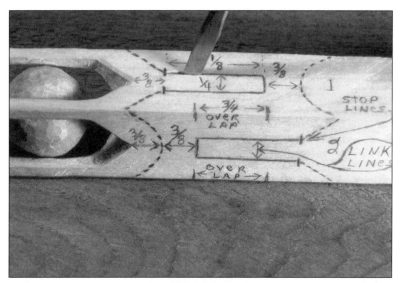

*Photo #6*

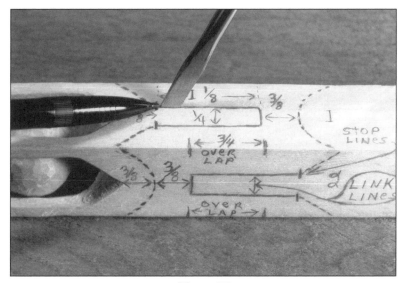

*Photo #5*

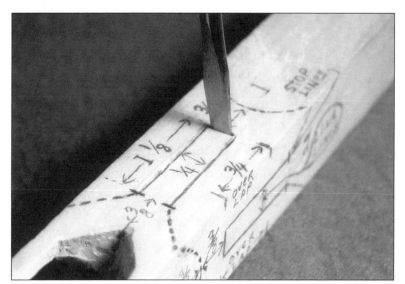

*Photo #7*

**How to Whittle the Whimsies of Yesterday**

The cut will have to be made deeper, but that will come later. In Photo #7, I made the cut to the end of the link and now am making the end of the link cut which is a cross-grain cut, much harder than cutting with the grain.

In Photo #8, I have almost finished the straight-in cut around the link lines on Side #1. Don't forget to make the cut only ⅛" deep from where the blade is to the stop line (where the pencil is pointing). Making the cut too deep here will leave a cut showing when the link is finished.

Photo #9 shows the straight-in link line cuts to a depth of ¼", except near the stop lines. These straight-in cuts are dangerous if you hold the piece in your hand. I recommend a safety glove on the hand holding the work piece. The safest way to make these and all the straight-in cuts is to lay the work piece on a non-slip surface, such as a piece of chamois or leather that is tacked to the workbench.

In Photo #10, I rotated the work piece ¼ turn and started the straight-in cuts on Side #2, beginning at the stop lines as we did on Side #1.

Start off by making the cuts ⅛" deep where the pencil is pointing.

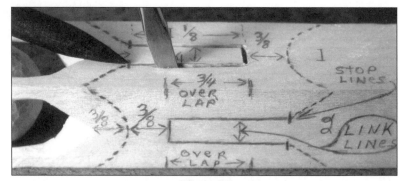
*Photo #8*

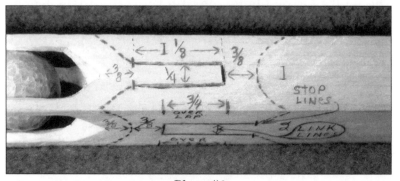
*Photo #9*

*Photo #10*

**How to Whittle the Whimsies of Yesterday**

Cut a bit deeper as you cut around the link lines and shallower as you near the other stop line. As you can see in Photo #11, the straight-in cut has been made. We have now finished the straight-in cuts on Sides #1 and 2. The cuts on Sides #3 and 4 will have to be done the very same way. With the link line cut straight-in on all four sides, we are ready to do some real whittling and ready to use the dotted lines that have been an eyesore for these last few pages. Use a knife with a stationary blade for whittling and deepening the cuts on the half-links.

Start whittling at the dotted lines as I have done on Photos #12 and #13. Making a cut on each end of the dotted lines will prevent a split in the wood that could ruin your whimsy. Whittling slowly, remove the wood right up to the straight-in cuts, being careful not to cut into the links.

*Photo #12*

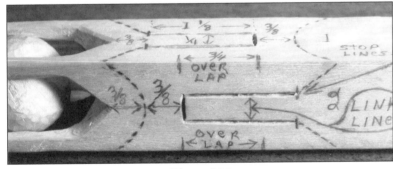

*Photo #11*

*Photo #13*

**How to Whittle the Whimsies of Yesterday**

From Photo #13 to #14, I have whittled away the unwanted wood, removing it right up to the straight-in cuts of the link. This step will be repeated on all four sides. So now, my whittling buddy, get started whittling the other three sides to look just like this side.

Well, my friend, that was whittling at its best and it didn't take but a few minutes. We now have all four sides whittled down to the link cuts, so I am wondering what to do next. I can still see wood between the end of the link cuts and the round dotted lines. What say we remove that wood and then see what our project looks like.

Wow, just a few chips really changed the looks! When making these four cuts, be careful not to split the end of the link. We only made the straight-in cuts ¼" deep, so you will have to deepen them as you remove wood.

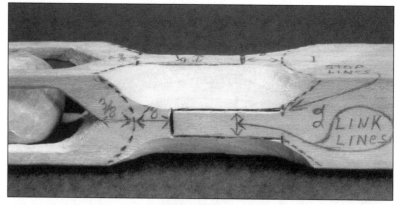

*Photo #15*

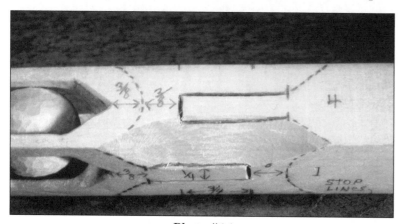

*Photo #14*

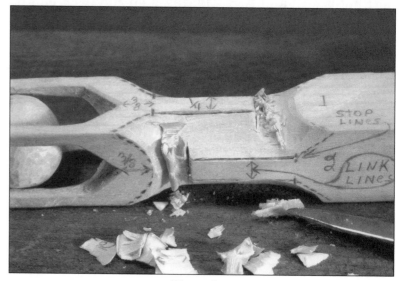

*Photo #16*

**How to Whittle the Whimsies of Yesterday**

I can tell you that the $3/16$ #7 gouge sure does work well for this kind of carving. You can do the straight-down cuts better with the gouge than with a knife. Note the cut on the right in Photo #17 is cut straight down to the side of the other link. When using the gouge always wear a safety glove. What's next? We have whittled from the dotted lines down almost even with the link on the opposite side.

The wood that remains in our way now would be a perfect trian-

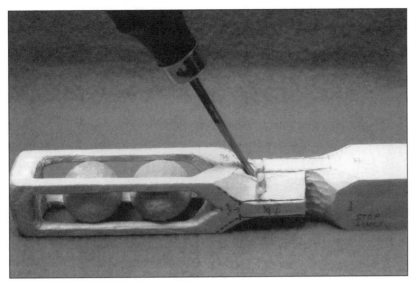

*Photo #17*

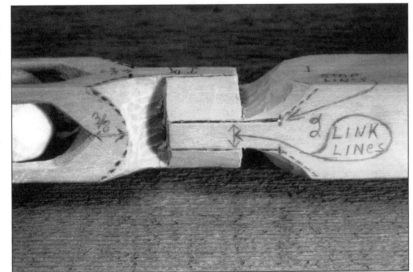

*Photo #18*

gle if we could remove it with one straight-in cut. That would be too hard to do without breaking our million dollar project, so I suppose we had better do it like they did in the old days, one small chip at a time.

Our straight-in cuts are about $1/4$" deep on all the link sides and what we have left to be removed is the overlap wood. Very soon now the overlap wood will be small chips in a towel in our lap. How about that for a little bit of wit?

We can start removing the overlap wood where the dotted lines are (where I have inserted the knife blade in Photo #19.) Remember the straight-in cut was already ¼" deep, so we can snap these bits of unwanted wood off on all four sides of the links. Proceed then to deepen the cuts and snap off some more unwanted wood until we have all four of our links looking like the one in Photo #21. After getting the link sides cleaned up, they should be approximately ⅜" tall, ¼" wide and 1⅛" long, if you measure from the stop line to the end of the link.

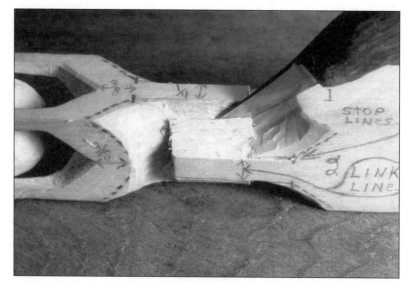

*Photo #20*

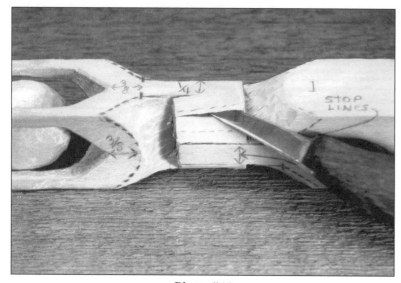

*Photo #19*

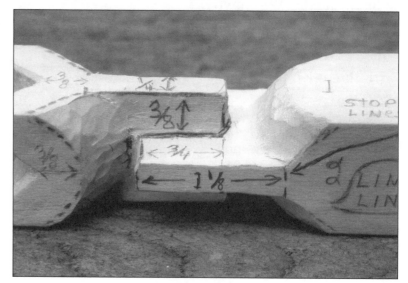

*Photo #21*

**How to Whittle the Whimsies of Yesterday**

Now, my friend, this is where the numbered sides come into play. Earlier I mentioned Sides #1 and #3 were to be drawn the same. So, too, are Sides #2 and #4 to be drawn the same. These shaded areas I have drawn on each side are where the wood will be removed, forming a hole through to the opposite side. From Photos #22 through 26, I rotated the work piece to show all sides in their entirety. Shade where the wood is to be removed, as I have done in these photos. Note where the pencil points in Photos #23 and #24. This is a small overlap where the X holes will be drilled to start the separation process.

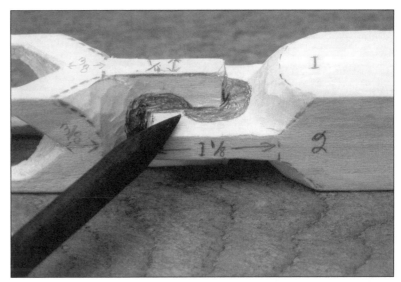
Photo #23

Photo #22

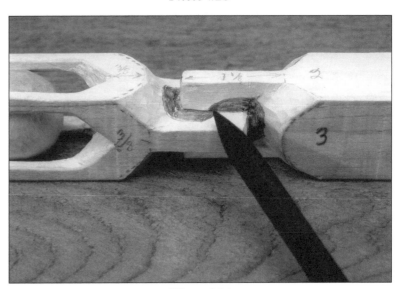
Photo #24

**How to Whittle the Whimsies of Yesterday**

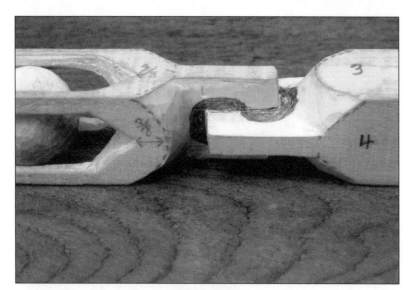

*Photo #25*

I had been whittling for years before it dawned on me that drilling the X holes would make this cut a lot easier. If you do not use a drill in making this cut, you will have to leave more overlap in Photos #22 through #26, where the pencil points.

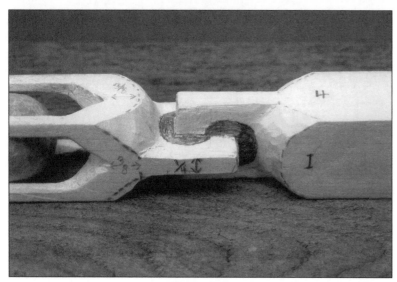

*Photo #26*

**How to Whittle the Whimsies of Yesterday**

The two pictures here are both drilling the same hole, but they are shown from different angles. I only drill the holes about halfway through on all four sides. If you drilled all the way through at the wrong angle, it would result in a hole through a link. The drawing here shows what we are trying to accomplish. As you can see, the angle on the lower left, if drilled all the way through, would come out in a side of the link. So drill in from all four sides and if you are lucky, you can feel the drill bit hit a hole you have drilled from the other side.

*Photo #28*

*Photo #27*

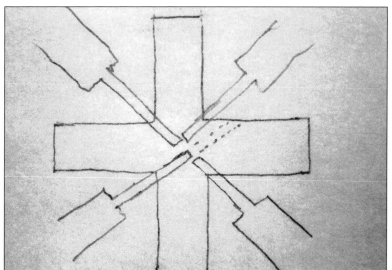

*Photo #28-A*

If all your X holes didn't meet good enough for the drill bit to line up with the hole on the other side, that will be okay for now. In Photo #29, I am doing a straight-in cut all the way around the shaded area, on Side #1. Cut only to $\frac{1}{16}$" deep and dig out the unwanted wood.

In Photo #31, I have made the straight-in cuts around the shaded area and now am making the cut around the link, digging our way through from Side #1 to Side #3, keeping the end of the link straight as we go.

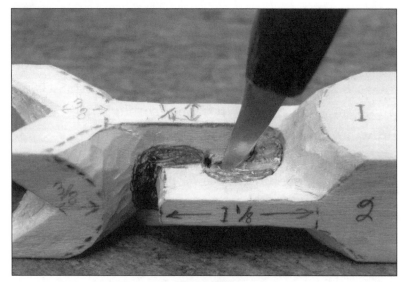

*Photo #30*

*Photo #29*

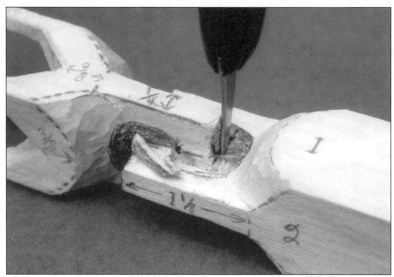

*Photo #31*

**How to Whittle the Whimsies of Yesterday**

*Photo #32*

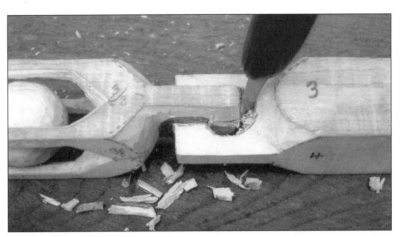

*Photo #34*

When the blade breaks through to Side #3 as shown in Photo #33, turn the work piece over and finish the hole from Side #3. The cut is almost made in Photo #34, just cleaning up a few fibers to finish the hole.

With all the wood removed around the link, this hole is complete. We are now ready to cut our way from Side #2 to Side #4. Note how the X holes show up in Photos #33 and #35.

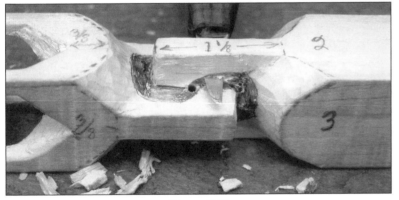

*Photo #33*

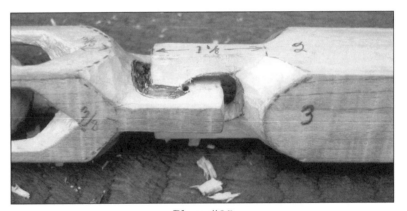

*Photo #35*

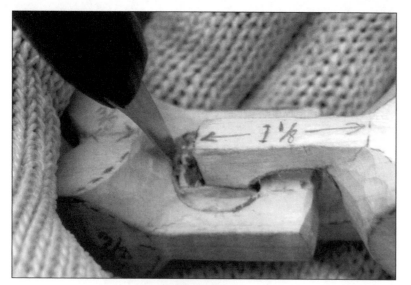

*Photo #36*

Here I am starting the cut from Side #2 to Side #4 using the safety glove. The link in this stage is easily broken. I support it in my hand and whittle very carefully to prevent a poke in the hand and keep from breaking the work of art. In Photo #37, the cut is about halfway through. In Photo #38, I have just pushed through to Side #4. We are now ready to work from side #4 and clean out the remaining wood.

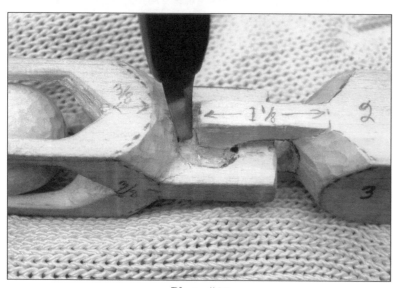

*Photo #37*

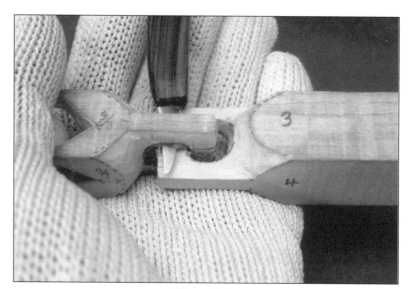

*Photo #38*

**How to Whittle the Whimsies of Yesterday**

*Photo #39*

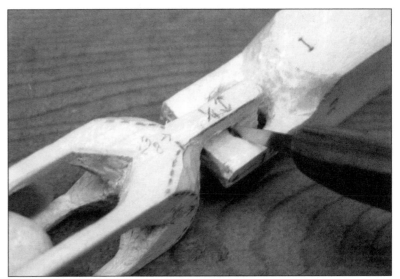

*Photo #40*

In Photo #39, the shaded holes have been completed. The only thing holding the link together at this point is the wood that remained after we drilled the X holes. Above I am using the hand drill to drill the wood between the X holes. Drill these holes no deeper than ⅛" Then, as is shown in Photo #40, cut the fibers that are left holding the link together. Bingo! The link is now free. Use the safety glove while making all these cuts. To get better pictures, I left the glove out of these pictures. When the link is separated, as in Photo #41, we are ready to start rounding off the corners.

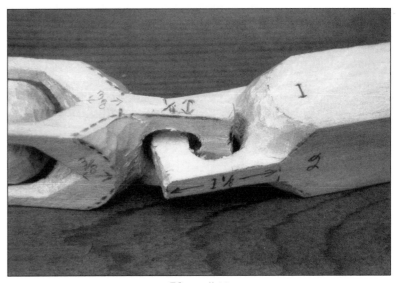

*Photo #41*

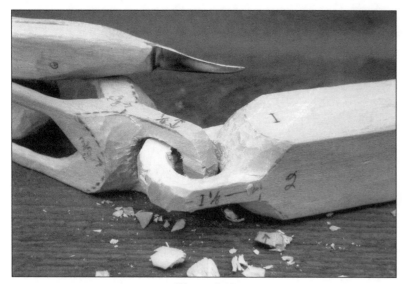

*Photo #42*

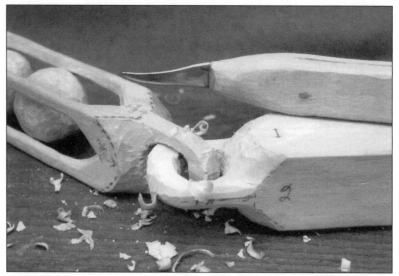

*Photo #43*

The sharp, thin bladed knife is needed to smooth up the inside curve of the link. Well, my whittling compadre, we could call the Joining Links finished (in Photo #44), but let's spend another hour or so just putting the finishing touches on our masterpiece.

*Photo #44*

**How to Whittle the Whimsies of Yesterday**

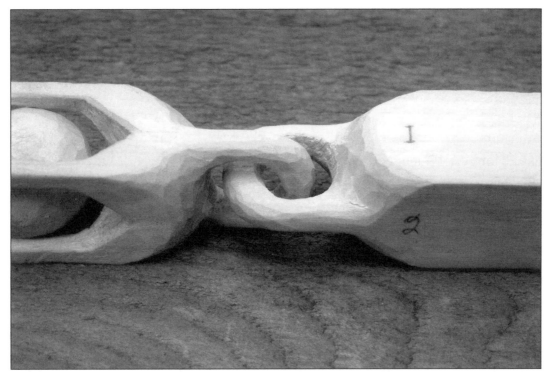

*Photo #45*

This is the Finished Link. I have whittled and trimmed just enough to remove the dotted lines, but have left the numbers on the sides, which we will use in the next step.

# The Slider

The slider, or slip joint, when finished, will make your whimsy almost 2" longer. This of course depends on how far apart the loops are. I have made a slider some 2 foot long before. The first few I did were completely whittled with a knife, making the slider bars round (shown with the finished slider), but for me to be able to show in detail, I used a scroll saw to cut away the unwanted wood. I have left the numbers on the sides for clarification.

As with the Joining Links, Sides #1 and 3 will be drawn the same and Sides #2 and 4 will be drawn the same.

The two photos shown here are actual size. Use tracing paper, trace Side #2 for a pattern to use in the next few steps, because when I saw away the unwanted wood in Photo #1, the drawing on Side #2 will be gone.

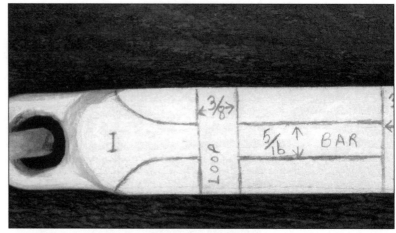

*Photo #1, Side #1*

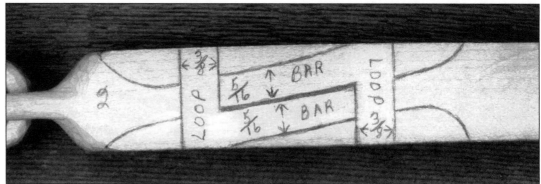

*Photo #2, Side #2*

On Side #1 in Photo #3, I have shaded the part to be cut away. In Photo #4, the shaded area has been sawed away. This cut can be whittled, but sawing shows more clearly the parts as they resemble a puzzle.

In Photo #5, the patterns we traced off Side #2 are ready to be placed back on Side #2 and redrawn.

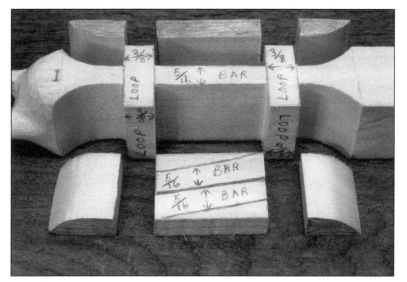

*Photo #4*

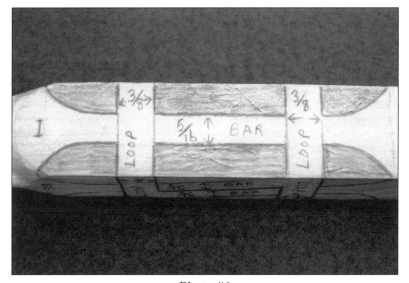

*Photo #3*

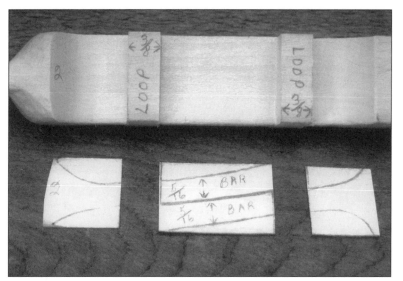

*Photo #5*

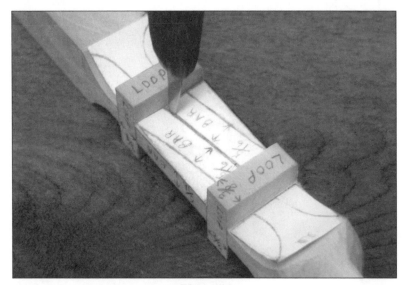

*Photo #6*

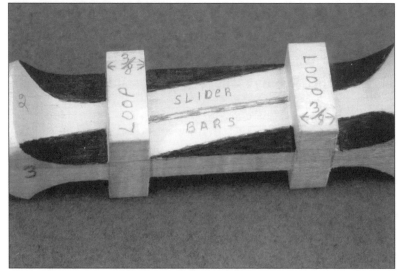

*Photo #8*

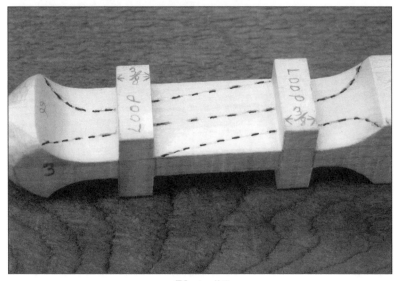

*Photo #7*

Photo #6 shows the patterns lightly glued in place. Take a sharp, pointed knife and punch holes through the paper, following the lines. Make the holes about $\frac{1}{8}$" apart and $\frac{1}{16}$" deep.

In Photo #7, I have removed the pattern and marked the tiny holes to make them more visible.

In Photo #8 (Side #2), I have shaded the parts which will be whittled away. I have dotted a line where the straight through cut will be made to divide the slider bars.

**How to Whittle the Whimsies of Yesterday**

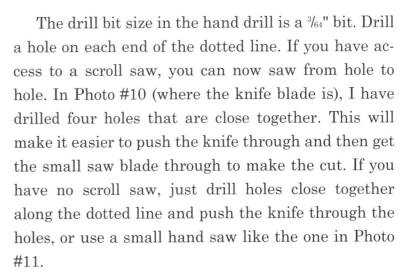

*Photo #9*

The drill bit size in the hand drill is a ³⁄₆₄" bit. Drill a hole on each end of the dotted line. If you have access to a scroll saw, you can now saw from hole to hole. In Photo #10 (where the knife blade is), I have drilled four holes that are close together. This will make it easier to push the knife through and then get the small saw blade through to make the cut. If you have no scroll saw, just drill holes close together along the dotted line and push the knife through the holes, or use a small hand saw like the one in Photo #11.

*Photo #10*

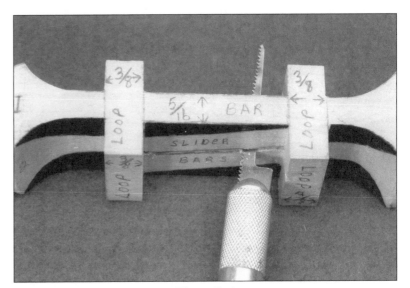

*Photo #11*

In Photo #12 the center cut has been made and we are almost ready to start whittling away the unwanted wood. Photo #13 shows Side #4, which is a mirror image of Side #2.

The pencil in Photo #14 shows the marks where we will cut straight down to form the loop. The X on the other loop means no cut will be made there. On the other side of the X, I have started the straight-in cut (where the knife blade is). In Photo #15, I have started whittling away the unwanted wood.

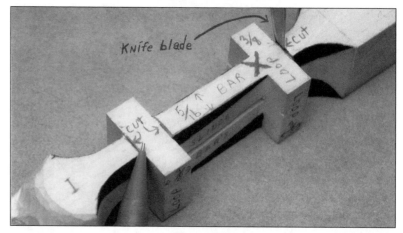

*Photo #14*

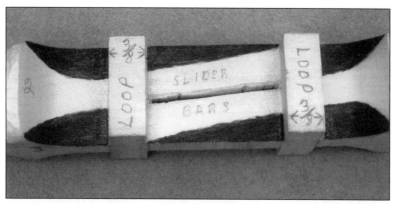

*Photo #12*

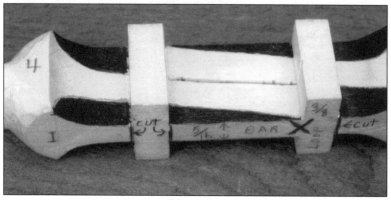

*Photo #13*

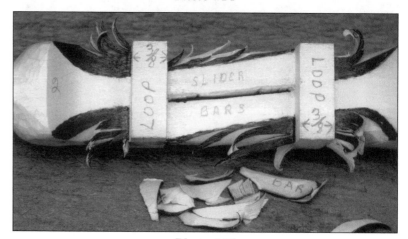

*Photo #15*

How to Whittle the Whimsies of Yesterday

With almost all the unwanted wood whittled away in Photo #16, we are about ready to start the loop separation cuts.

In Photo #17, the wood has been whittled to the place where all we need now is a hole through each loop around the slider bars. Where the pencils are pointing, I have shaded the area where the cuts will be made. These cuts are a bit different from the chain link cuts we have made. We will use the sharp, pointed knife, the hand drill, and a small saw.

*Note*: the upper pencil is pointing to the inside of the loop. (The inside of the loops are only shaded on three sides.) The lower pencil is pointing to the outside of the loop. (The outside of the loops are shaded on all four sides.)

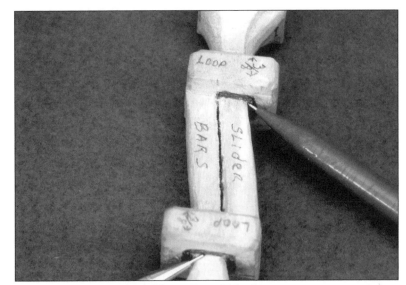
*Photo #17, Side #2*

*Photo #18, Side #1*

*Photo #16*

**How to Whittle the Whimsies of Yesterday**

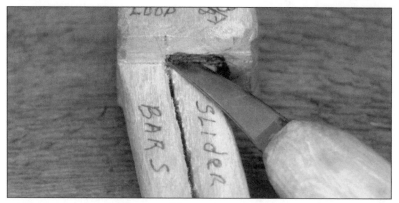

*Photo #19*

In Photos #19 and 20, I am pushing the point of the blade into the loop, about $\frac{1}{8}$" deep, staying flat against the slider bars. (Wear the safety glove while making these cuts.) Make these straight-in cuts on both sides of both links (where the shading is). This cut is with the grain of the wood and is easy to do, but

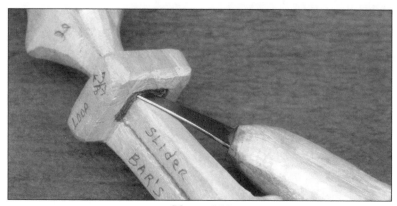

*Photo #20*

do not try to push the knife completely through the loop as this will split the loop.

After these cuts are made, start back around at an angle as I show in Photos #21 and 22. When you have both sides of both loops whittled out, there should be only about $\frac{1}{8}$" of wood left to be removed. Remember the X holes and the hand drill? In Photos #23 and 24, we bore through the wood we couldn't get to with the knife.

*Photo #21*

*Photo #22*

**How to Whittle the Whimsies of Yesterday**

Drill the X holes around the three sides of both loops. This will create enough room to slip the knife blade through, and then the saw will remove the fibers that are left. This leaves us with one cut remaining: that is to free the loop from the slider bars. That is the continuation of the cut between the slider bars. (See photos #9 through #11.)

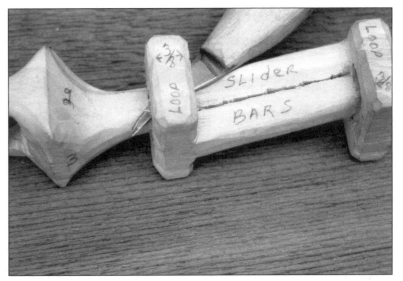

*Photo #25*

*Photo #23*

*Photo #24*

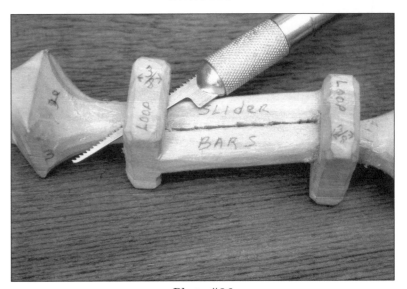

*Photo #26*

**How to Whittle the Whimsies of Yesterday**

To finish the cut between the slider bars and the loop, we have to drill the X holes as shown in Photo #27.

Drill these holes on both loops. This will get us started on making the continuation cuts. Note that the drill bit went through at the right place. This is important. If the angle is off, you may drill through the loop or into the bar.

Now turn the work piece over to Side #4 and drill holes like we did on Side #2. Be sure the drill bit goes through at the right place. If in doubt, drill through from the other side as we did when drilling the X holes for the chain links.

The pencil is just a reminder to drill X holes through both ends of the continuation cuts.

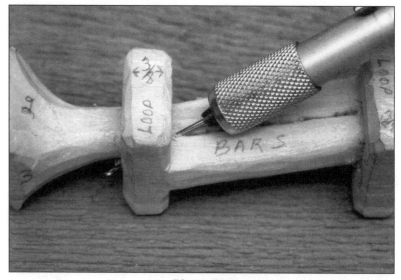

*Photo #27*

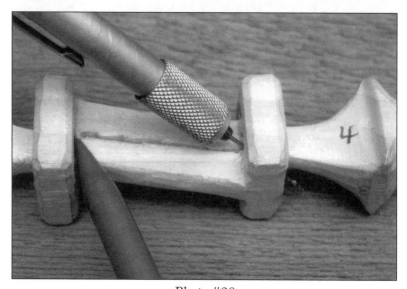

*Photo #28*

**How to Whittle the Whimsies of Yesterday**

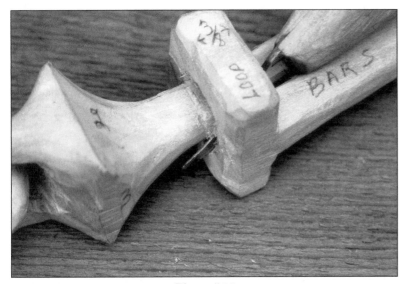

*Photo #29*

Drilling the X holes has created just enough space between the bar and the loop to gently push the thin, sharp bladed knife through. Work and push the knife very carefully so as not to break your whimsy.

Work the blade through each of the X holes, enlarging them on both loops. When you finish this set of cuts, you should begin to feel the loops start to separate from the bars. You may have to go all the way around each loop, freeing any remaining fibers still holding the loops to the bars. Now it is almost free.

*Photo #30*

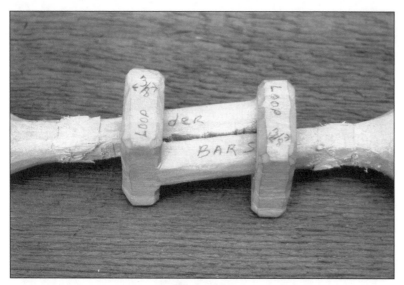

*Photo #31*

When the loops break free from the bars, you will have such a great feeling of accomplishment. This event will rank up there with other events in your life like the first time you rode a bike by yourself, the first time you drove a car without your Mom or Dad, your first swim, etc. . . . . It is quite a thrill!

In Photo #31, the loops and the bars are free to slide. They are rough at this stage and it shows how much work you put into this wondrous piece of art.

Nothing left to do now but clean up the rough places on the bars.

In Photo #32, I have one bar cleaned up and doing the other bar as you read this page.

*Photo #32*

**How to Whittle the Whimsies of Yesterday**

*The finished Slider*

*My first Slider*

This is the Finished Slider with the writing whittled off and enlarged. The bottom photo is my first slider attached to a ball in a cage shown in actual size.

It was whittled with an Old Timer knife sometime in 1980s. I regret now that I didn't date it, so you be sure and date all your projects.

**How to Whittle the Whimsies of Yesterday**

# The Split Chain

The first section of the Split Chain is very similar to the Basic Chain. The main difference is that the chain is smaller with less overlap and the numbers are placed around the edges of the slope going down to the slider bars.

To help with the layout, I have a drawing beside the work piece showing the slope, the ⅝" distance from the slope to the dotted line and the 4" to the midsection line.

**Step #1**: Number all four sides close to the slope and keep all the numbers in the same order as the Slider's numbered sides. Example: #1 (Chain side the same as #1 Slider Side.) Sides #1 and #3 will be on opposite sides and drawn exactly the same.

Sides #2 and #4 will be on opposite sides and drawn exactly the same.

**Step #2**: The dotted lines. Measure ⅝" from the slope and draw a dotted line straight around the block. This is to line up the stop lines and the link line ends.

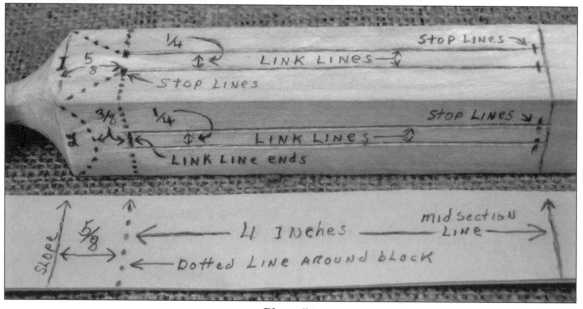

*Photo #1*

**How to Whittle the Whimsies of Yesterday**

Pencil in the stop lines on Sides #1 and #3. Draw the link line ends on Sides #2 and #4. We are now through with the dotted line (around the block) and it can be erased.

On Sides #1 and #3, from the stop lines, dot the lines back to the corners of the slope. On Sides #2 and #4 dot a curved line, as shown, ³⁄₈" from the link line ends back to the corners of the slope, intersecting with the straight lines on Sides #1 and #3.

**Step #3**: From the stop lines and the link line ends that we have just drawn, measure 4" down the block, as shown in Photo #1, and draw the midsection line around the block. This is where the chain will split. Now draw the midsection stop lines ¹⁄₈" from the midsection line, as shown.

**Step #4**: The link lines on this section of chain will not have the cross on the end like the Basic Chain did. Draw the link lines as shown on Sides #1 and #3, from stop line to stop line ¹⁄₄" apart.

On Sides #2 and #4, you will draw the link lines

*Photo #2*

from the link line ends to the midsection stop lines ¹⁄₄" apart.

**Step #5**: Make the link line cuts on Sides #1 and #3 (with the screwdriver knife or the round pointed knife) and make the straight-in cuts ¹⁄₄" deep getting shallower as you get close to the stop lines.

As shown in Photo #3, I am using the ³/₁₆" screwdriver knife to make the link line cuts. As I approach the stop lines, I bring the cut up and stop the cut about ⅛" from the stop line. When you have the link line cuts made on Sides #1 and #3, turn the work piece over to Side #2.

*Photo #4*

In Photo #4, I am making the link line cuts on Sides #2 and #4. I am starting at the midsection stop line with the ³/₁₆" screwdriver knife to make the long link line cuts. On the link line end cut, I use the ⅛" screwdriver knife or a small round pointed knife because it is a narrow cross grain cut. It requires a small blade.

*Photo #3*

**How to Whittle the Whimsies of Yesterday**

*Photo #5*

**Step #7**: Removing the waste wood. Where the pencil is pointing is where we made the midsection cuts. I first removed a small amount of wood here, so as not to split off a corner of the block. I then started at the dotted lines whittling away the waste wood toward the pencil, since the link line cuts have been made. These will now become link bars so be careful not to cut into a link bar.

**Step #6**: Making the midsection cross grain cut. I have erased the stop lines close to the midsection line and have made the straight-in cuts around the block *but not across the Link Lines.* These are hard cuts to make, so lay the work piece on a nonslip surface and cut them as deep as the link line cuts. They will need to be deepened as we deepen the link line cuts. As shown, these cuts are about ⅛" inside the midsection line.

*Photo 6*

**Step #8**: In Photo #7, I have whittled away the wood on all four sides right down to the link bars, like I started showing in Photo #6. With the gouge I have made the cut from the dotted line on Sides #2 and #4 around the link bar end. On the Basic Chain we did these cuts starting at the cross, but here on the split chain there is no cross on this section of the chain.

*Photo #8*

*Photo #7*

When making the cut around the end of the link bar, keep it squared up as shown in Photo #8. Side #2 will be carved around the link bar exactly the same way. To deepen the straight-in cuts in Photo #8, I use the store bought skew. You must take care when doing these straight-in cuts and not go too deep because it must still be an almost perfect cross even though we can't see the cross on the end.

**How to Whittle the Whimsies of Yesterday**

When all the waste wood in Photo #8 has been removed, then we are ready to draw the chain layout.

**Step #9**: The Basic Chain only had one half link or joining link. The Split Chain will have two half links on each end of the chain. Each full link will be 1¼" long. The half links will be approximately ¾" long, the hole through the joining links (shaded area) will be ½" long, and the hole through the full links is ¾" long.

On the Basic Chain I went into greater detail with the layout. If in doubt, look back at the Basic Chain. The overlap on the Basic Chain was ¼" and this chain is ¹⁄₁₆" overlap. The distance between the links was ¼" and here they come together. Remember that Sides #1 and #3 have to be drawn exactly the same as will Sides #2 and #4.

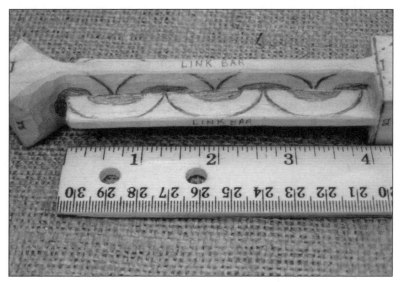

*Photo #9*

In Photo #9, Side #1 is on top and Side #2 is facing the camera. If you turned Side #3 up, then Side #4 will be facing the camera and will look exactly the same. Before I began writing this book, I never once drew the layout on the wood. It is much harder for me to draw the layout than to whittle it!

In Photo #10, Side #2 is on the top and Side #3 is facing the camera. If you turned Side #4 up with Side #1 facing the camera, it will look exactly the same.

Photo #11 shows Side #1 facing the camera. Side #3 is on the opposite side and is drawn exactly the same.

Photo #12 shows Side #2 facing the camera. Side #4 is on the opposite side and is drawn exactly the same.

Before I make any cuts that I have doubts about, I may spend a lot of time pondering it, sharpening or honing my knives, or even sleep on it overnight. After all, we are making a one-of-a-kind and unique whimsy here and we have already spent a lot of time on it.

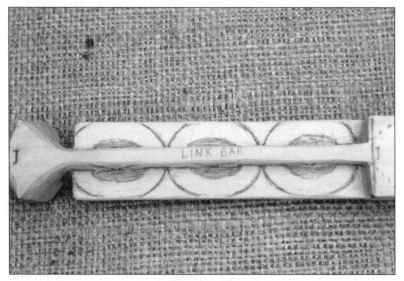

*Photo #11*

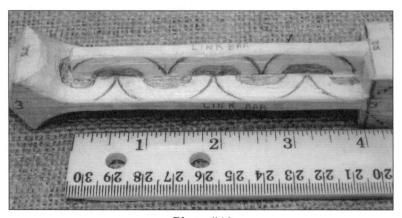

*Photo #10*

*Photo #12*

**How to Whittle the Whimsies of Yesterday**

**Step #10:** Laying out the link that will split the chain into two ½" chains. This will be a joining link or half link on the single chain side like the ones we have already done on the basic chain, and drawn on this chain. The sides are still numbered the same on all four sides.

As with all the chains and joining links, each op-posing side will be drawn exactly the same as shown in these four photos.

The drawing beside the joining link shows the measurements from the midsection line. ⅜" to the right of the midsection line on Sides #2 and #4 put a straight dotted line. On Sides #1 and #3, draw the dotted lines to intersect with the link bars and the straight dotted lines on Sides #2 and #4.

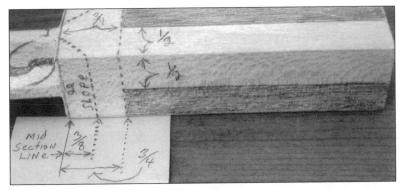

*Photo #13*

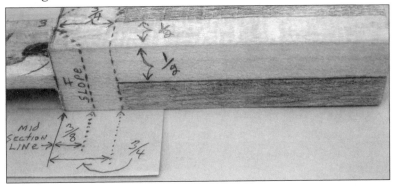

*Photo #15*

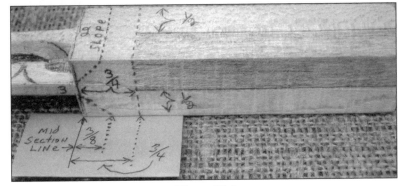

*Photo #14*

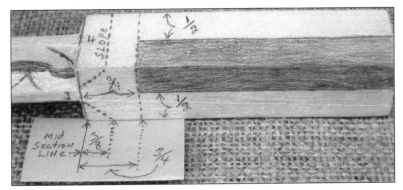

*Photo #16*

**How to Whittle the Whimsies of Yesterday**

The second dotted line is drawn all the way around the block, ¾" from the midsection line. And from the dotted line around the block, I have divided each side of the block into ½" sections and have shaded the right-hand side. Photo #17 shows the end of the block with Side #1 on top. The shaded side will be removed.

**Step #11**. Photo #18 is where I start the straight-in cuts that will separate the shaded area and the non-shaded area. Start these cuts at the end of the block and stop them ⅛" from the dotted line, as shown.

I have also began whittling away the unwanted wood or waste wood to make the slope down to the link end of the 1" chain. In Photo #19 the slope cut is made and I have drawn in the shaded area around the link end (where the pencil is pointing).

*Photo #18*

*Photo #17*

*Photo #19*

**How to Whittle the Whimsies of Yesterday**

**Step #12**: Removing the waste wood from the shaded areas. In Photo #20 I am whittling the shaded area down to the straight-in cuts. In Photo #21, I am deepening the straight-in cuts so that I can remove the remaining unwanted or waste wood, leaving the un-shaded area.

Photo #22 shows that all the unwanted or waste wood has been removed therefore leaving two separate ½" square blocks. They measure 3¼" long from the dotted line.

*Photo #21*

*Photo #20*

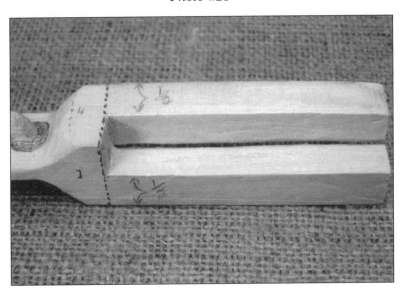

*Photo #22*

**Step #13:** I have crossed out one block as we can only do one at a time. In Photo #23 the midsection line and the dotted line have been whittled away and from the original dotted line I have drawn a new dotted line ¼" to the left which we will use later on. Now you will number the sides, keeping the same number on the same side as the one shown in the 1" chain layout.

In Photo #23, Side #1 is facing the camera and Side #4 is on top. In Photo #24, Side #1 is on top and Side #2 is facing the camera. Side #3 is on the bottom or the opposite side of Side #1, and Side #4 is on the opposite side of Side #2. Whew! Believe me I am no rocket scientist and if I can figure this out, so can you.

In line with the original dotted line, draw the stop lines on Sides #1 and #3. The little lines by the stop lines are where the cuts get shallower. Now draw the link lines ⅛" apart to the end of the block and the little angled dotted lines from the stop lines to the new dotted lines (where the two little arrows are pointing on Side #1 in Photo #23).

On Sides #2 and #4 draw the link line ends (where the little arrow is pointing in Photo #24). Side #4 will be drawn exactly the same. Now draw the link lines

to end of the block and form the cross on the end, just like the Basic Chain.

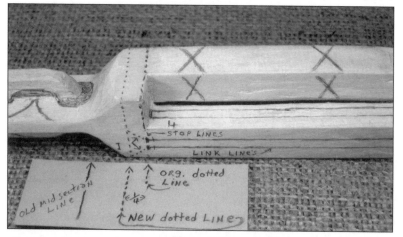
*Photo #23*

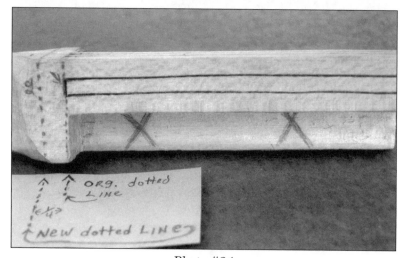
*Photo #24*

**How to Whittle the Whimsies of Yesterday**

In Photo #25 we are now ready to do the straight-in cuts on the link lines starting at the cross and cutting to the stop lines on Sides #1 and #3. Cut to the link line ends on Sides #2 and #4, making the cuts about ⅛" deep and make the link end cuts. The ½" block under the work piece will support the work piece while making the cuts on your non-slip surface.

**Step #14:** Remove the waste wood from the cross to the stop lines and the link line ends. In Photo #26 the unwanted or waste wood has been removed below the link bar on Side #2 and I am deepening the straight-in cut above the link bar (where the medium pointed knife blade is). The dark arrow shows where I have rounded off the corner of the block removing about half of the dotted line on Side #2 and whittling down to the block with the two Xs on it.

What remains of the new dotted line on Side #2 is now the slope line where the cut will start sloping down to the link bar end (where the little arrow is pointing).

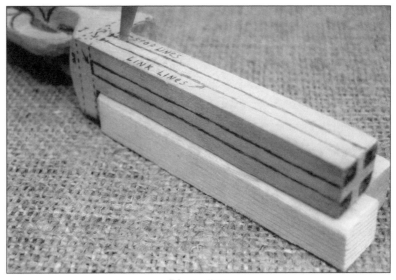

*Photo #25*

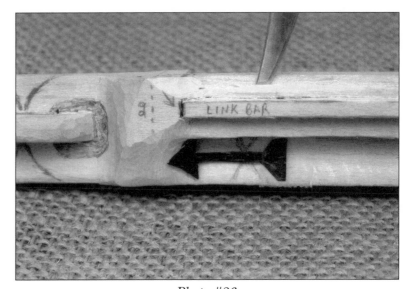

*Photo #26*

Photo #27 shows the slope cut made down to the link bar end. They are link bars when they reach this stage. All the waste wood has been removed on Side #2 and the shaded area drawn in around the link bar end. Now let's turn the work piece to Side #4 and make it look exactly like Side #2.

In Photo #28 on Side #4, I carefully make the cut around the link bar end (where the knife blade is). There is very little room to work, so the thinner the knife blade the better. I also use the small hand drill to help with this cramped, no-room cut. With persistence, you will prevail. The pencil is pointing to the corner of the block that I have whittled away and then drawn the new dotted lines. Compare this photo to Photo #23.

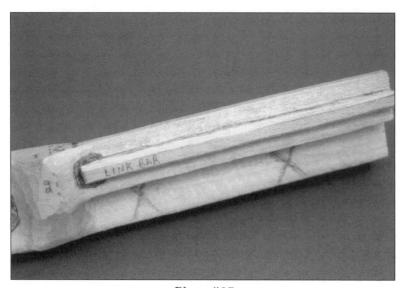

*Photo #27*

*Photo #28*

**How to Whittle the Whimsies of Yesterday**

In Photo #29, the cut to square the end of the link bar has been made, and the area for the hole has been shaded. This cut is very tedious, but hang in there—if it was easy everybody would be doing it.

Photo #30 shows that from the point of the arrow down to the shaded area, around the link bar end, that it slopes down almost ½".

Photo #31 shows the link bars are finished and ready to be made into a chain. So now let us make the joining link cut.

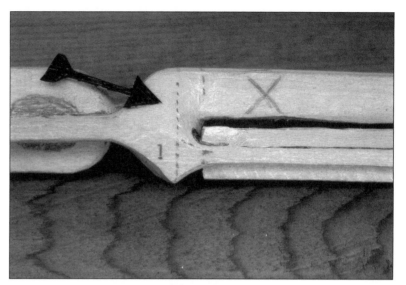

*Photo #30*

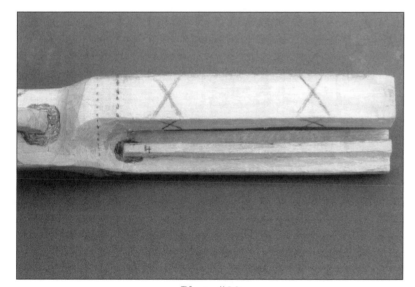

*Photo #29*

*Photo #31*

*Photo #32*

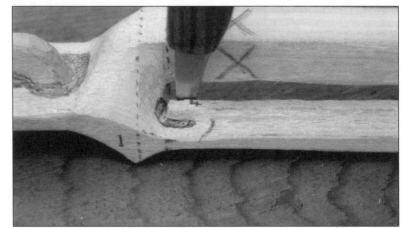

*Photo #33*

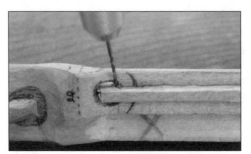

*Photo #34*

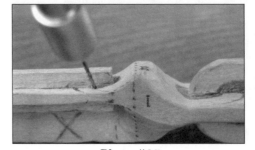

*Photo #35*

**Step #15**: Joining the ½" chain to the 1" chain. We haven't whittled out the 1" chain yet. The little chain is easier to whittle first as we can use the 1" chain for a handle while we are whittling the little chain.

Photo #32 shows cutting the hole for the half link. Cut around the link bar end with the straight-in cuts. This chain is much thinner than the big chain and therefore it is easily broken. Wear the safety glove and support it in your hand. Side #4 has very little room to make the cut shown in Photo #33, so go slow and be patient. It just takes time.

When you have the hole cut through the shaded area drill the X holes. Drill only about halfway through so that you won't ruin the link on the other side. Side #4 cannot be drilled from just one angle, so dig gently as this also just takes time.

**How to Whittle the Whimsies of Yesterday**

*Photo #36*

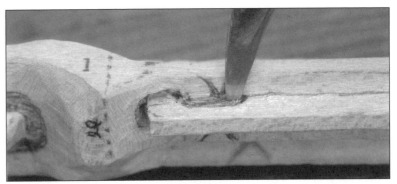

*Photo #37*

*Photo #38*

Photo #36: draw the next shaded area.

Photo #37 Make the next shaded area cuts from Side #1 through to Side #3. Support your work piece in the hand that is wearing the safety glove.

Photo #38 You will need to round off the corners (where the pencil is pointing) and then make the separation cuts. You will need to make very small cuts since this chain is easily broken while making this cut.

Photo #39 shows the separation cuts made and the link bars free to swing out away from the other ½" block. This gives us plenty of room in which to work now. Personally I think it is easier to lay out the chain one link at a time. After a dozen feet of chain you will probably not even use a pencil to draw the links . . . just whittle them.

*Photo #39*

**How to Whittle the Whimsies of Yesterday**

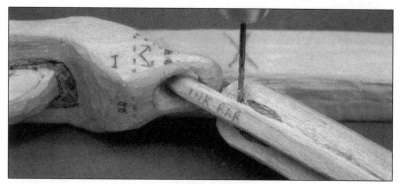

*Photo #40*

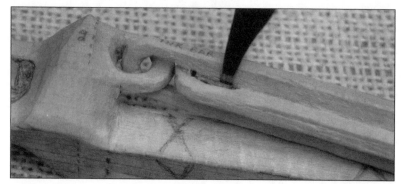

*Photo #41*

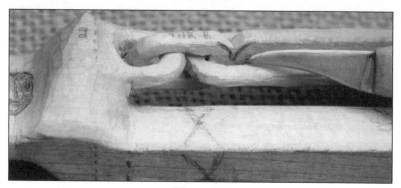

*Photo #42*

**Step #16:** Photo #40 shows the half link cleaned up and the X holes being drilled for the next link. Shade the area where the hole will go through. I have made the shaded areas a little shorter than I think it will take, but you can always make them longer if needed.

Photo #41 Do the straight-in cuts. Dig halfway through, turn to the opposite side and dig through until the cuts meet.

Photo #42 shows that the hole is made through the shaded area, the marks are drawn and the separation cut is half-made to free the first link.

Photo #43 shows that the link is free but still needs some clean up whittling and shaping.

*Photo #43*

**How to Whittle the Whimsies of Yesterday**

*Photo #44*

*Photo #45*

*Photo #46*

**Step #17: The Procedure.** Drill the X holes using a $\frac{3}{64}$" or smaller bit in the hand drill. As shown in Photos #44 and #45, drill halfway through on all four sides and then shade the area for the next hole. Do the straight-in cuts around each shaded area as shown in Photo #46. In Photo #47 the hole is completed through the shaded area and I am using a spiral scroll saw blade which has been glued in a wooden handle to clean out the fibers inside the hole. Note how the X hole shows up. The X holes are not the complete cut. They only make it easier to work the thin sharp pointed knife blade through to finish the cut.

*Photo #47*

**How to Whittle the Whimsies of Yesterday**

*Photo #48*

As shown in Photo #48 you need to work the blade in at this angle between all the X holes, cutting the wood that the drill bit doesn't cut. When the X hole cut is complete, then draw the lines for the separation cut.

In Photo #49 the separation cut is about halfway done. This is a simple whittling cut, but must be supported by your safety gloved hand. Do not force any of these cuts, but instead make little shaving cuts, rounding the link as you whittle it free. Focus on the link rather than getting it centered in the hole. See Photo #48. You can make the hole longer if needed for the next link.

Photo #50 shows that the link is free and whittled clean. This link procedure is complete, so proceed in this order to the end of the block with the X holes and the shading being the next step.

*Photo #50*

*Photo #49*

**How to Whittle the Whimsies of Yesterday**

Photo #51 is a look back at what we have done so far. We have come a long way but still like a few more days. Don't abandon ship now.

*Photo #51*

**Step #18: The Next ½" Block.**

Erase the Xs we put on when we started the first block. Position your block like the one here in Photo #52 and number it the same way. Side #1 is facing the camera, Side #2 is on bottom, Side #3 is on the opposite side and Side #4 is on top. This will give us the same numbering system as the first block but different from the 1" chain.

On this block we will have the Joining Link, the two links of chain and another Joining Link joining the chain to a cage with a two pointed spear inside.

In line with the original dotted line, draw the stop lines on Sides #1 and #3 and the link line ends on Sides #2 and #4. (Refer to Step #13.) Everything will be done the same except for the length of the link lines. Here on bar #2, draw the link lines only 1¼" long, leaving the ends open.

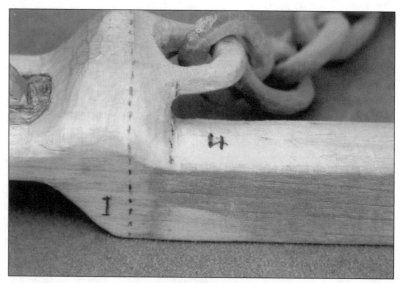

*Photo #52*

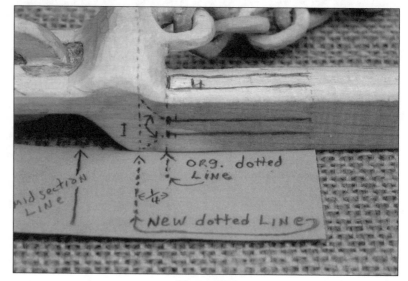

*Photo #53*

**How to Whittle the Whimsies of Yesterday**

*Photo #54*

*Photo #55*

In Photo #54 I have made all the link line cuts making the cuts shallower as I got close to the stop lines on Sides #1 and #3. The link line end cuts are made on Sides #2 and #4. We are now ready to remove the wood around the short link line cuts turning them into link bars.

Photo #55—you will make a cut where the pencil is pointing and start whittling at the dotted lines toward the pencil. Make these same cuts on all four sides, but do not cut across the link bars on the end where the pencil is pointing in Photo #55.

In Photo #56 all four sides have been whittled down to the straight-in cuts. The slope cut will start where the pencil is pointing down to the link end cut.

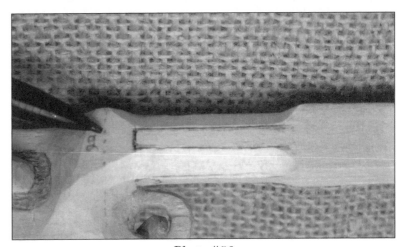

*Photo #56*

**How to Whittle the Whimsies of Yesterday**

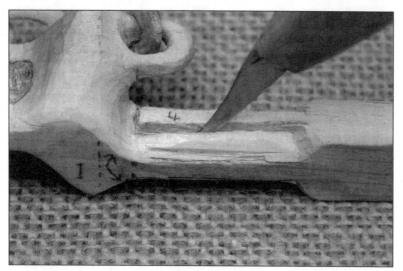

*Photo #57*

Photo #57 shows where we are deepening the straight-in cuts and the end of the link bar cuts (Photo #58) and removing the unwanted wood to get it ready to make the shaded area cut on the half link as shown in Photo #59. This is the same cut as shown in Photo #32 and #33 on the other ½" block. The only difference is that here on block #2 the link bars do not go to the end of the block. Repeat Steps #15 and #16 (Photos #32 through #43).

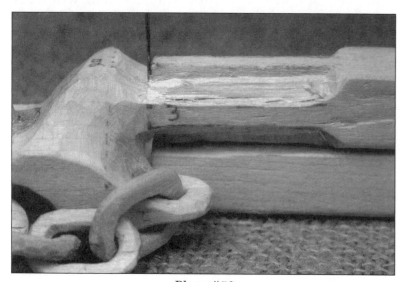

*Photo #58*

*Photo #59*

How to Whittle the Whimsies of Yesterday

*Photo #60*

*Photo #61*

*Photo #62*

In Photo #60 I have repeated Steps #15 and #16 to get to the same stage on block #2. The black pencil is pointing to the link that we have cut free and done the cleanup whittling on. The silver tip pencil is pointing to the link end mark where we will make the straight-in cut. From the dotted line on Sides #1 and #3 we will make the slope cut just like we did in Photo #58 on Side #2.

In Photo #61 the slope cut is made on Sides #1 and #3.

The X hole cuts can now be made as shown in Photo #62. Round the corners off and draw the shaded area for the half link cut.

Photo #63 shows the straight-in cut being made around the shaded area where we will dig through from Side #1 to Side #3.

*Photo #63*

**How to Whittle the Whimsies of Yesterday**

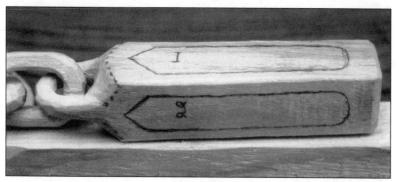

*Photo #64*

*Photo #65*

*Photo #66*

Photo #64. Here the half link cut is complete and we are ready to do the finishing touches on the split chain.

**Step #19: The Two-Pointed Spear.**

The ½" block in Photo #64 is 2" long from the curved dotted line on Side #1 to the end of the block. From the point of the cage to the dotted line is ¼".

From the oval end of the cage to the end of the block is also ¼", making the cage 1½" long.

The cage bars are drawn ³⁄₃₂" from the edge of the block or the thickness of two quarters as shown here in Photo #65. The quarters show how small the block is and because it is so small it is hard to hold while making the straight-in cuts.

In Photo #66 I use a 1"×4" piece of scrap wood and two ½"×½" pieces of wood attached to the 1"×4" to lay the work piece in while I make the straight-in cuts. This will serve two purposes. One: it will prevent a bad cut. Two: it will help in keeping the work piece from splitting when we make the straight-in cuts.

**How to Whittle the Whimsies of Yesterday**

In Photo #67 you will make the straight-in cuts only ¹⁄₁₆" deep on all four sides. I use the small knife shown in the Knife section in Photo #36 to make the straight-in cuts. The screwdriver knife is too blunt to make these very small and fragile cuts.

The Two-Pointed Spear is done very similar to the Football in a Cage. It is on a much smaller and delicate scale and will look a lot different when finished.

In Photo #68, the pencil is pointing to the side cut which is only ¹⁄₁₆" deep and will not get much deeper. The ends are about ¹⁄₈" deep. When we get all four sides looking like Side #1, then we will start to shape our spear.

Side #2 is cut to the right depth but the ends haven't been gouged out like Side #1. I use a ¹⁄₈" #3 gouge for the ends. Be very careful because the small gouge is a dangerous little guy. We learn by doing, or at least I did.

Now it seems our whimsy is too long to lay in my lap and position it properly in the cradle on the 1"×4", so I decided to make the half link cut on the 1" chain so that it would fold in the middle, thus making it much easier to handle.

In Photo #69 I am starting the straight-in cuts on the half link of the 1" chain.

*Photo #67*

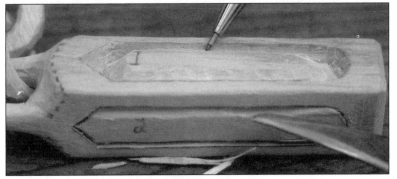
*Photo #68*

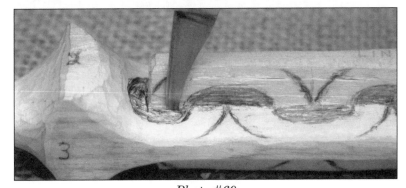
*Photo #69*

In Photo #70 the hole is through the half link and I am making the X hole cuts.

Photo #71 shows making the straight-in cuts on the next link and digging out the unwanted wood.

Photo #72 is making the separation cut.

Photo #73 shows that by folding the whimsy in the middle, it will be a lot easier to lay the ½" block in the cradle to finish the two-pointed spear.

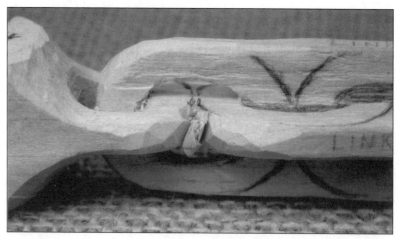

*Photo #72*

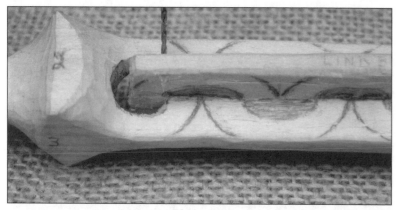

*Photo #70*

*Photo #73*

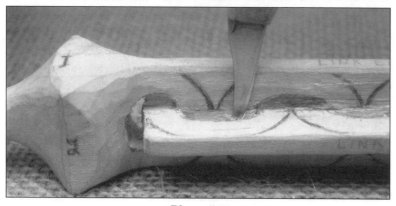

*Photo #71*

**How to Whittle the Whimsies of Yesterday**

From Photo #68 to Photo #74, I have shaped the two-pointed spear to the stage where it looks almost like the Football in a Cage. See Photos #10-12 in the Football in a Cage section.

In Photo #75 the ends and the midsection (where the stripe is) are still attached to the block. This gives it strength while we finish shaping it. The points will be the last places we cut free.

Photo #76 shows shaving the inside of the bars just a little bit and whittling the center of the spear to be free of the bars as in Photo #77.

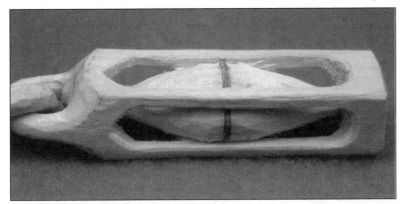
*Photo #74*

*Photo #76*

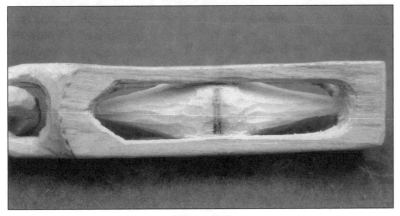
*Photo #75*

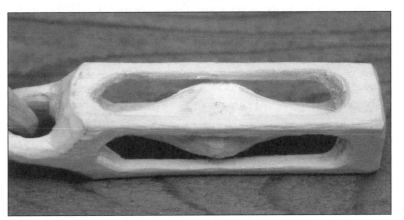
*Photo #77*

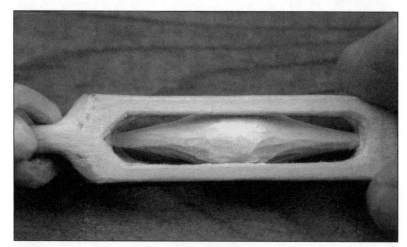

*Photo #78*

In Photo #78 the points are the only thing holding the spear in place. Note how small it is compared to my fingers.

When the points are cut free, you will still have to whittle the spear until it will turn crossways in the cage. This is not hard to do but takes about an hour or two of whittling. Take small shavings and make the center part of the spear round like a ball, as shown in Photo #79.

We have thus far on this 18" long, 1"×1" piece of Bass wood, whittled Two Balls in a Cage, two Joining Links, The Slider, another connecting link, and drawn five links of a 1" chain (which we have not whittled out yet), The Split Link with the two ½" chains, one with the two pointed spear. All that we like having this whimsy finished is whittling out the 1" chain. Let's sharpen our tools and finish this masterpiece. Remember to sign it, date it, and of course tell everyone how easy it was to make.

*Photo #79*

## Step #20: Finishing the 1" Chain.

When you catch a severe case of whittling fever, I am sorry to say that there is no known cure (unless it was discovered while this book was being printed).

In Photo #80 one link is free on the 1" chain.

Photo #81 shows me shaping the next link before cutting it loose. This will give you a handle to hold while working on it.

In Photo #82 we are out of handle and have whittled our way to the dividing link. When this is done our whimsy is finished and it has been two barrels of fun!

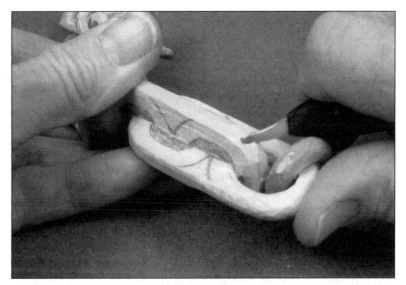

*Photo #81*

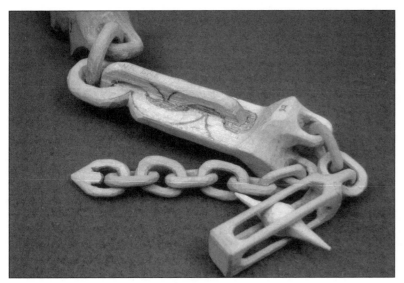

*Photo #80*

*Photo #82*

# The Lollipop Behind Bars

This will introduce how to get acquainted with the swivel using the form of a lollipop behind bars.

This is a 1½" square block of Bass wood that is 6⅛" long. Remember in the introduction that I said to never throw away a small piece of wood in case you might want to make a small whimsy. Well, this piece was in an assortment box and it just happened to be this size. Any size would work for this Lollipop Behind Bars just as long as you keep the measurements in proportion.

In this piece of wood the cage is 2⅞" long. The Cage bars are ³⁄₁₆", the ball is 1⅛" in diameter, the spindle will be ⅜" going through a ¾" piece of wood (where the dotted lines are).

Leave ½" on the right end for strength. When you have finished drawing the layout, then the first step will be the straight-in cuts.

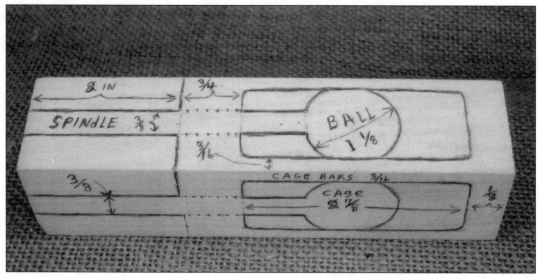

*Photo #1: The layout for the Lollipop*

**How to Whittle the Whimsies of Yesterday**

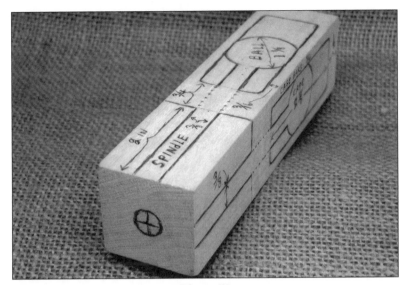

*Photo #2*

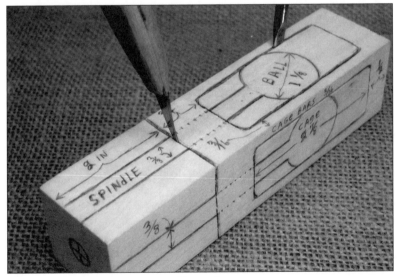

*Photo #3*

Photo #2 shows the end view. Find the center and draw a ³⁄₈" circle, as the spindle will be whittled down to the size of the ³⁄₈" circle.

In Photo #3, for making the straight-in cuts with the grain, I use the screwdriver knife. For making the cuts across the grain, I use the medium pointed knife.

As you can see in Photo #3, I have made all the straight-in cuts and have started removing the unwanted wood. The Lollipop Behind Bars will be whittled like the Balls in a Cage until you get it to the point of whittling the spindle. You don't want to cut too deep here. *The swivel is a different and new kind of whittling, so follow the photos and go slow.*

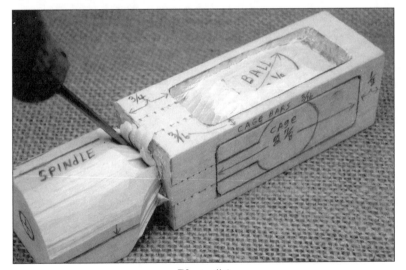

*Photo #4*

**How to Whittle the Whimsies of Yesterday**

Photo #5: Whittling the Lollipop stick down to size. I use the ³⁄₁₆ gouge to get to the size of Photos #5 and #6 and then use a knife to whittle the stick down to size like in Photo #7.

Note the dotted lines in Photo #7. Put these lines on all four sides. Center them up ³⁄₈" apart. This is where the cut must go through. Turn the work piece, looking at all four sides. The stick (or spindle) must be lined up inside and out. Here in Photo #7, I still like a little having the stick whittled small enough. So it's back to turning and whittling, turning and whittling, until . . .

*Photo #6*

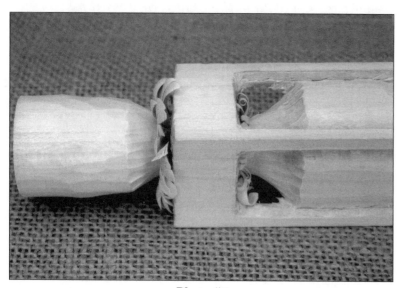

*Photo #5*

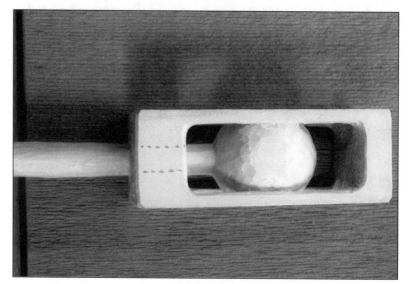

*Photo #7*

**How to Whittle the Whimsies of Yesterday**

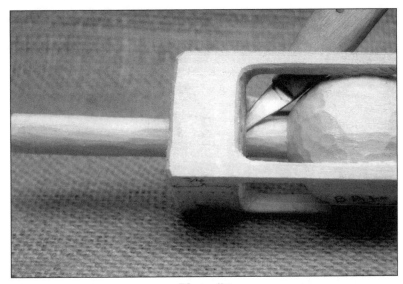

*Photo #8*

The stick is the right size and appears to go straight through the block where the dotted lines are. That is what it will do when we get the hole cut around it so it can slide back and forth.

As in Photo #8, you will work the knife in beside the stick all the way around about ¼" deep, inside and out.

In Photo #9 and #10 use the ⅛" gouge to cut in at the angle shown but don't go too deep and cut into the stick. Leave the ball attached to the bars until this cut is made. (Photo #9 where the arrows are pointing.)

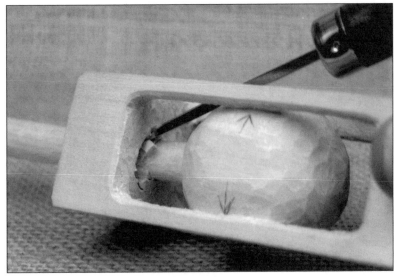

*Photo #9*

*Photo #10*

When you finish with the gouge in Photos #9 and #10, you should have only ⅛" wood left around the Lollipop stick. Take a long, thin blade and work it through the remaining wood as shown in Photo #11.

When you have worked the blade through in several places, the small saw (shown in Photo #12) will cut the remaining fibers and the stick will be free. It will still need to be whittled clean after we cut the Lollipop free from the bars.

Now you will whittle the Lollipop down about ⅛" smaller in diameter so you can free it from the bars.

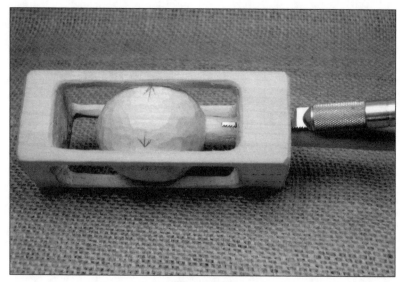

*Photo #12*

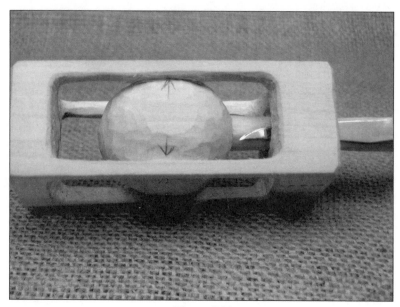

*Photo #11*

*Photo #13*

**How to Whittle the Whimsies of Yesterday**

Now your Lollipop will slide up and down in the cage but it won't come out. It will, however, be a bit hard to lick and that is why we put it behind bars so that you wouldn't get splinters in your tongue! So with that little bit of fun, our Lollipop is done.

*Photo #14: The finished Lollipop*

As this book goes to print, I am working on the advanced *How to Whittle the Whimsies* book. So until we can whittle together again, keep your knives sharp and stay in practice. You might try your hand at some of the projects shown here: The Ball in a Ball on a

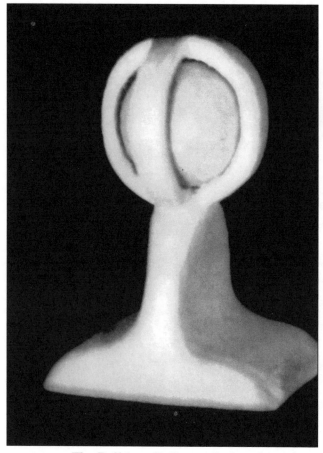

*The Ball in a Ball on a Pedestal*

*The Tower of Balls in a Cage Crowned with a Heart*

*An Arrow Through the Heart*

Pedestal, The Tower of Balls in a Cage Crowned with a Heart, an Arrow Through the Heart, and a Doughnut on a Stick in a Cage.

*In the next book you will be amazed by what we will do.*

Happy Whittling,
JACK D. JACKSON

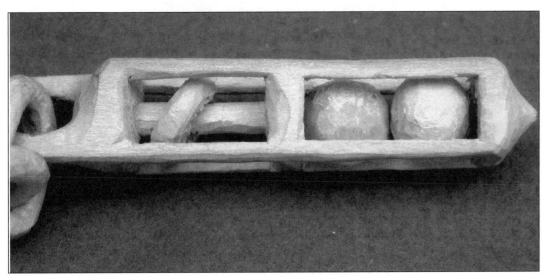

*Doughnut on a Stick in a Cage*

We all, I guess I have a weakness or two. I must confess I have four—whittling, the great outdoors, a campfire, traveling, and fishing. Oops, seems I miscounted, make it five.

There's an old German proverb that says something to this effect: Contentment is worth more than riches. These weaknesses of mine bring an abundance of contentment!